Funny Peculiar

A Directory of the Daft and Dotty

Other titles by Aubrey Dillon Malone

The Cynic's Dictionary
Historic Pubs of Dublin

Funny Peculiar

A Directory of the Daft and Dotty

Aubrey Dillon Malone

PRION

First published 2001 by
Prion Books
An imprint of the
Carlton Publishing Group
20 Mortimer Street
London W1T 3JW

Reprinted 2005

ISBN 1-85375-460-9

A catalogue record for this book can be obtained
from the British Library

Index compiled by Emily Bradshaw
Jacket design by Carroll Associates

Printed and bound in Great Britain by
Mackays, Chatham

ABSENT-MINDEDNESS

Sir Isaac Newton (1642-1727)

The great scientist was notoriously absent-minded. One night when he was entertaining guests, he went to his wine cellar to get a bottle and forgot to come back. Instead he wandered to chapel, ruminating on a scientific problem that was bothering him. He once even used his fiancée's finger to crush the tobacco into his pipe.

Rev. George Harvest (1728-89)

This vicar from Surrey seemed incapable of remembering that he was meant to get married. He forgot to go to church on his own wedding day, spending the day fishing instead. When he decided to re-marry towards the end of his life, he again forgot to go to church, spending the day with friends. His absent-mindedness wasn't, however, limited to nuptials: he would often write a letter to one person, address it to another and post it to a third. And when visiting friends in the evening, he would sometimes wander upstairs and get into their beds, imagining he was at home.

Thomas De Quincey (1785-1859)

Possibly as a result of his early opium addiction, De Quincey was incredibly absent-minded and prone to setting his hair on fire while he was working. He also once borrowed seven shillings and sixpence from a friend and gave him a note as security. When his friend smoothed out the screwed up piece of paper he had been given, he discovered it was a £50 note.

Robert Cecil Salisbury (1830-1903)

This former British Prime Minister was once at a cere-mony when he noticed a young man smiling at him. Asking a colleague who he might be, the politician received the answer 'Your son'.

G.K. Chesterton (1874-1936)

The writer and critic, who won the public over with his amiable detective-priest in *The Innocence of Father Brown*, was prone to unusual absent-mindedness: he was often to be espied in the middle of the road deep in thought or laughing at some private joke as cars whizzed by on every side of him. On his wedding morning he blacked his face, washed his boots in hot water, poured coffee on his sardines and put his hat on the fire to boil.

W.B. Yeats (1865-1939)

The Irish poet was so absent-minded he often put sugar in his soup and salt in his coffee. He was particularly forgetful when writing poetry: almost to the extent of failing to recognise the world around him. This reached its extreme the day he passed his daughter Anne in the street and enquired of her, 'Pray, what is your name?'

Frank O'Connor said Yeats was so besotted with his art that, in the middle of a conversation, he would lift his right hand and beat time with it as he recited a few of his lines. Then he'd go back to the conversation as if nothing had happened.

William Wilkie (1721-72)

Scotland's unpredictable poet was also a preacher, though not a very effective one. He was so absent-minded that he sometimes forgot to consecrate the bread and wine at Mass, and once even left the church in the middle of a service, totally forgetting that he was conducting it.

ANIMAL CRACKERS

Cyrus the Great (600-529BC)

The Persian emperor sentenced a river to death when his favourite horse drowned in it.

Mohammed (570-632)

The founder of Islam had so much reverence for cats that he once cut off the sleeve of his coat rather than disturb a cat that was sleeping on it.

Lord Holland

This peer, who lived in the time of William III, used to arrange musical concerts for his horses. He organised one concert per week for his 200 steeds, fervently believing they mellowed the horses' moods.

Peter the Great (1672-1725)

The Russian emperor brought ten spaniel dogs to bed with him when he was training them to hunt. He had a greyhound called Lisette to whom he was devoted. When one of his courtiers was accused of corruption, his wife tried to intercede on his behalf. Peter refused to listen to her imprecations until she tied the plea round Lisette's neck. Then he was won over.

Francis Henry Egerton (1736-1803)

Egerton, the 3rd Earl of Bridgewater, was one of Britain's more colourful 18th-century figures, if only for the attention he lavished upon his pet dogs Bijou and Biche. He dressed them in silk coats, satin breeches and handmade leather boots, and had linen napkins placed round their necks when they dined with him so that their 'clothes' wouldn't become soiled if they dribbled. Footmen attended their every need, following them about with umbrellas if they ventured outdoors on rainy days.

Jemmy Hirst (1738-1829)

This tanner from Doncaster first showed his affection for animals by riding a pig that his headmaster kept at school. In time, the enterprising Jemmy even trained it to jump hurdles. In later years he went hunting on the back of his bull, Jupiter, accompanied by a dozen pigs he trained to act as gun dogs. He became something of a legend in the Doncaster area and was even invited to dine by George III. Jemmy, however, declined because he had a previous engagement: he was training an otter to fish.

Jeremy Bentham (1748-1832)

Philosopher, jurist and social reformer, Bentham once conferred a knighthood on his cat, calling it 'Sir John Langhorn'. The 'Sir' became 'Reverend' after he decided to ordain it. When it died, he organised a lavish funeral for it in his garden.

Charles Waterton (1782-1865)

A whimsical old squire who belied his great wealth by dressing in rags and sleeping on the floor with a block of wood for a pillow, Waterton was fascinated by animals from youth and made it his life's plan to capture as many as possible. As he intended to stuff them, he had to kill the animals cleanly. He wrestled with alligators, snakes and boa constrictors. He would sometimes contort the animals' features when he was stuffing them to shock scientists who came to view his collection.

His interest in animals went beyond stuffing them, however. On one trip to London Zoo he climbed into a cage with an orang-utang. Onlookers thought he would be savaged but man and animal seemed to have a mutual sympathy for each other. As he wrote afterwards: 'He took hold of my wrist and fingered the blue veins therein contained, while I myself was lost in admiration at the protuberance of his enormous mouth. He most obligingly let me open it and thus I had the opportunity of examining his two fine rows of teeth.' A moment later the pair of them were embracing like long-lost brothers.

Waterton also liked to give his animals the chance to communicate with one another and built his stables in such a manner that his horses could 'converse' in their stalls. He kept a donkey as a pet, riding it around his mansion for years before eventually making it a pensioner on his estate.

Lord Byron (1788-1824)

When he was at Cambridge, the university had a rule against students keeping dogs or cats, so the resourceful poet decided to buy a trained bear instead: there being nothing in the regulations to prohibit pet bears.

Jack Mytton (1796-1834)

This outlandish squire had a veritable menagerie of animals, including more than 2000 dogs and 60 cats. He dressed the latter in livery. He rode his horse not only into hotel rooms but also up staircases and, on one occasion at least, jumped from a balcony down onto a street without injuring either himself or the steed. He named one of his children Euphrates after his favourite horse.

He was fond of playing pranks on his guests and once rode into his dining room on the back of a brown, female bear (called Nell) – giving the assembled gathering the fright of their lives. He went one step further at another party and put his bear into bed with a drunken reveller. It was the next morning before the hapless imbiber realised who his bedfellow was.

Gerard de Nerval (1808-1855)

The French poet was noted for taking his pet lobster for walks around Paris, especially in the gardens of the Palais Royale, on a lead. When asked why, he replied, 'Because unlike dogs, they can't bark at you'.

Florence Nightingale (1820-1910)

The so-called lady with the lamp was said to have owned sixty cats and also a small owl that she kept in her pocket at all times.

Frank Buckland (1826-80)

This naturalist kept live snakes and mice in his pockets. He was threatened with eviction from a coach once when it was discovered he had twelve live tree frogs about his person. The authorities didn't discover the slugs he was also hiding in his pockets, which escaped when he fell asleep. On waking, he saw one of them crawling across the bald head of a passenger sleeping opposite him and decided to make himself scarce.

Buckland kept animals in his home as well as his pockets and had a large collection of stuffed animals and also many living creatures. He had a raccoon, an owl, a buzzard, monkeys (which were prone to bite his guests), a chameleon, a mongoose, numerous snakes and a pet bear which he dressed in a scholar's cap and gown. The bear eventually ended up in London Zoo after being caught trying to rob a sweet shop. He had a monkey which he dressed as a troop corporal until he discovered it had been ripping the buttons off his coat. He then demoted it to the status of private, with suitable sartorial adjustments.

In 1861 Buckland took to fish-farming and set up a museum of fish culture in South Kensington which so impressed Queen Victoria that she invited him to visit her. In 1867 he was appointed Inspector of HM Salmon Fisheries and had to travel all over England, ensuring that salmon could get past all the man-made obstacles in waterways, such as weirs, and reach the sea. At one point he left the salmon a note which read: 'No road at present over this weir. Go downstream, take the first turn to the right and you will find good travelling water upstream and no jumping required. F.T.B.'

The fact that he constantly smelt strongly of fish meant that he was often given his own carriage on trains. When he died, a note was found in his will stating that as God was so good to the little fishes, he would also protect their inspector, continuing 'I am going on a long journey where I think I shall see a great many curious animals...'

Sir Thomas Barrett-Leonard (1857-1918)

This Essex squire instructed his workers to keep a fresh bowl of water in the corn rick for the enormous rats that took up residence in his home, much to the distaste of the other members of his household who lived in fear of their meals being snatched from under their noses by the pampered rodents. He also refused to hunt the deer that proliferated round his grounds. When he was travelling in his carriage, he sometimes got out and walked if he felt his weight was making the journey arduous for his horse.

Albert Schweitzer (1875-1965)

The German theologian, philosopher and musician made a decision in 1896 that he would devote his life to science and art until he reached the age of 30, at which point he would direct his attentions to serving humanity. He was true to his word and, in 1905, despite being a musician and theologian of international repute, Schweitzer began to study medicine and became a medical missionary, setting up hospitals to treat leprosy and sleeping sickness. He was also fond of animals and insects, and refused to kill even mosquitoes and ants if they appeared in his tent. His cat Sizi liked to sleep on his left arm, which was something of a problem for the doctor when he was writing prescriptions because he was left-handed. Rather than wake the cat, however, he would write with his right hand instead.

John Barrymore (1882-1942)

This actor, best known for his Shakespearean roles, kept a pet vulture which he fed on meat scavenged from other people's dustbins.

John Christie (1882-1962)

Founder of the Glyndebourne Festival Opera, Christie loved animals so much that he tinkered with the idea of building a dog cafeteria at the Opera House where dog-lovers could deposit their pets while the concerts were going on.

Raymond Chandler (1888-1959)

Doted on his cats, which were kept almost as advisers and 'consulted' on literary matters, going so far as to call one of them his secretary.

Edward VIII (1894-1972)

This monarch was so crazy about his dog Cora that he brought her up to bed with him every night. When his beloved animal developed rheumatism in later life, he had steps built so that she could get into the bed more easily.

Marion Davies (1897-1961)

This Hollywood actress and comedienne was so attached to her pet dachshund that she had an official funeral for him, presided over by a priest, when it died.

K.G. Gandar Dower (1908-44)

This British poet and explorer attempted to enliven the sport of greyhound racing in 1937 by replacing the hounds with cheetahs. He brought eight of them back after a trip to Kenya and everyone was agog as he lined them up for their first race. Alas, the cheetahs weren't as turned on by mechanical hares as the trained greyhounds and, after refusing to chase them, they were flown back to their natural habitat.

Marlon Brando (1924-)

Kept a pet raccoon in his New York apartment during his twenties. 'He's not only my best friend,' he told people, 'but my mistress as well'. He fed it with a baby bottle, slept with it nestled in the crook of his arm and even talked to it after it fell asleep.

Patricia O'Neill (1924-)

In December 2000 the Irish daughter of the Countess of Kenmare and sister of Lord Waterpark, at the age of 75 decided to write her husband Frank out of her will because she preferred her pet chimp Kalu. The chimp, whose favourite hobby is bashing Frank over the head, is set to inherit a cool £40 million when Patricia dies. Patricia also owns 22 baboons, six of which are babies who, at her insistence, have to share the marital bed to facilitate night feeds. She has 48 chimps, several peacocks and a handful of dogs as well. Her favourite of all of these, is Kalu, which she treats as a human being. He behaves like one as well, and is fond of smoking Frank's cigarettes and drinking his beer from the fridge. Patricia feels that by leaving her massive fortune to Kalu she will stop Frank getting his revenge on the chimp for its cheeky behaviour when she dies. As the situation stands, Kalu will live out the rest of his days peacefully on a luxury animal sanctuary.

George Armstrong Custer (1939-76)

The American soldier of 'Custer's Last Stand' fame was so fond of animals that he slept with beagles, staghounds, wolfhounds and foxhounds.

Edward Dorrell

This imaginative Shropshire farmer currently races not horses, not dogs, but sheep. And not only on the flat. No, these sheep, hatted and carefully numbered like thoroughbred steeds, actually jump fences, encouraged to maximum speeds by the promise of food at the end of the track, which is a furlong in length and has two turns and four fences. Each race consists of eight or nine runners, and there's a Sheep Grand National once a year, with the commentary coming from Edward (who's an ex-jockey) over a PA system. The sheep have names like Lucky Leggy, Larry Lamb and Hairy Harry. Some day, Edward hopes, the idea might catch on at Aintree or Fairyhouse.

ARRESTS

Grigori Rasputin (1871-1916)

After it was discovered that the Russian monk could cure the son of the Empress Alexandra of haemophilia, he gained considerable influence and was able to get away with almost anything in Russia. An inveterate trouble-maker and notorious for his womanising (some suggested he was even romantically involved with the Empress), Rasputin was once arrested for being drunk and disorderly in a bar. On being asked to confirm his identity by the police, he dropped his trousers and stuck out his penis as proof.

Enrico Caruso (1873-1921)

This Italian opera singer was once arrested by police for pinching a lady's *derrière* in the monkey house of a New York zoo.

Marquis of Waterford

The 19th-century Irish eccentric, noted for his reckless riding habits such as galloping up the stairs of the Kilkenny Hunt Clubhouse, was once arrested for riding the horse too fast, but he disputed the charge. In court, he rode his horse right up to the judge's bench and demanded that it be cross-examined: only it, he insisted, could know for sure how fast he was going.

Zsa Zsa Gabor (1919-)

Arrested in 1989 for punching a police officer in Beverly Hills after he pulled her over for driving with an out-of-date licence, she described her experiences at the police station as being like 'Nazi Germany' and excused her slap to the arresting officer by saying, 'I have a Hungarian temper'. She spent 72 hours in jail and had to pay $13,000 in court costs.

Brendan Behan (1923-64)

While on the Aran Islands he was arrested for being drunk and disorderly. Instead of going peacefully to his cell, he managed to disarm the two policemen and lock them up instead. The duo were the only policemen on the island, so afterwards he boasted of having imprisoned the entire police force.

Peter O'Toole (1932-)

Was once arrested by the police for breaking into his own home: he doesn't carry his own house keys, believing it to be unlucky, and no one else was in. Neither does he own a watch or wallet – so don't expect him to be punctual, or buy you a drink.

Wanda Ennis

After holding up a gas station in Louisiana in 1981, Wanda gave herself up for arrest unnecessarily after watching what she thought was a closed circuit TV coverage of the robbery. What she didn't realise was that the footage wasn't of herself at all but of a police-woman acting in a reconstruction.

Kevin Thompson

This criminal who held up a New Jersey bank in 1987 was caught and arrested because he wrote the hold-up note on the back of his pay cheque stub ... and forgot to ask for it back after the robbery.

Anthony Colella

American bank robber who was running down the street one day in 1989 with the takings from his latest heist when he was robbed. So he did the obvious thing: he reported the theft to the cops. But his arrest for the original robbery soon followed.

ARTISTIC LICENCE

James Whistler (1834-1903)

The opinionated artist was so obsessed with colour that he once dyed rice pudding green so that it would match the walls of his dining room.

Salvador Dali (1904-89)

Was once asked by his wife to paint a screen to put in front of an old radiator. When he did so, the design he chose was that of ... an old radiator.

William Turnbull (1922-)

Scottish abstract artist who won the princely sum of £3000 in an exhibition in Liverpool in 1978 for his painting 'Untitled': a blank canvas which, he advised helpfully, could be hung either way.

Andy Warhol (1928-87)

The Pop Art pioneer sometimes produced paintings by having his dog pee on his canvases. In 1949 he submitted a painting to the Pittsburgh Associated Artists exhibition that featured himself with his finger up his nose. It was entitled 'The Broad Gave Me My Face, But I Can Pick My Own Nose'.

Christian Boltanski (1944-)

This French artist held an exhibition in London that consisted of two tons of secondhand clothes. The public were charged £1 each for a carrier bag, into which they piled items of their choice.

Carl Andre (1935-)

American sculptor who held a one-day exhibition in 1973 of his latest creation which consisted of 500 pounds of cheese, ten inches thick, topped with ten gallons of ketchup.

Jean Verame (1936-)

This French artist painted a valley in the Sinai desert red, black and yellow in 1980. It took him six months to cover 70,000 square feet before conservationists took his brush away.

Fernandez Arman (1928-)

This French sculptor's *pièce de résistance* was a 59-foot-high structure which he exhibited in 1982. It consisted of 60 old cars encased in concrete and piled on top of each other.

Dennis Oppenheim (1938-)

An artist who went a bit beyond the call of duty for a photograph he entitled 'Reading Position for a Second Degree Burn' in 1982. To achieve the effect he wanted he lay under a blazing sun for hours, burning himself badly in the process. He placed an open book on his chest so that the rectangle under the book would remain white.

Joseph Ramsauer

Artist who won second prize in an Iowa exhibition in 1982 for presenting a large sheet of white paper with an adhesive bandage stuck on to it.

Ernie Cleverley

This Liverpool artist sold an abstract painting to a woman in 1983 for £70. When he revealed to her that it had been done not by himself but his pet duck, she demanded her money back. But Ernie held firm, claiming the duck was as talented as himself.

Chris Ofili (1968-)

An African artist who won the Turner prize in 1998 with pictures partly made up from elephant dung. Ofili started using dung he brought back from Zimbabwe on his canvases; he now gets his dung from London Zoo and dries it in an airing cupboard.

ARTISTS

Leonardo da Vinci (1452-1519)

Was so fascinated by ugly people he often followed them for hours.

John Ruskin (1819-1900)

The artist was so aghast at the sight of his wife's naked body on their wedding night that he fled the boudoir in terror. (Apparently he had never seen a woman's pubic hair before.) The marriage was never consummated, Ruskin preferring to masturbate obsessively. 'A suicide committed daily' he called it. He eventually went mad, running screaming from a university podium one day in mid-lecture.

James Whistler (1834-1903)

This American painter, dandy and wit carried two umbrellas if it was raining, just in case one of them broke. He wore black velvet pantaloons with diamond buckles and pink bows on the shoes, sometimes combining this with a white stove-pipe hat. If asked out to dinner, he frequently fell asleep at the table. When poverty hit him later in life his furniture was taken from his house. To console himself, he painted pictures of the absent items in the places in which they had once been situated.

Pierre Auguste Renoir (1841-1919)

Was so fond of nature he refused even to kill an ant, feeling this would upset the balance of things. According to his son Jean, it irked him so much if he happened to step on a dandelion unwittingly as he was walking through fields that he would swerve dramatically if he found himself approaching one the next time.

ARTISTS

Vincent Van Gogh (1853-90)

Van Gogh used to beat himself with a stick when his work didn't measure up to his expectations. He once tried to commit suicide by ingesting oil paints and kerosene when the painting was going badly.

Van Gogh was almost as obsessed with women as he was with painting. He cut off his left ear in 1888 out of frustration over the fact that his friend Paul Gauguin was more successful with a particular one. He handed it to her in an envelope and she fainted when she saw it. He painted a picture of himself after the mutilation entitled 'Self-Portrait with Bandaged Ear'.

Henri de Toulouse-Lautrec (1864-1901)

As a result of alcoholism, syphilis and depression, Toulouse-Lautrec was beset with hallucinations, most of which had him struggling with imaginary enemies like a savage pack of terriers, a monstrous headless elephant that prowled around his room trying to drive him against his bed, and even a cardboard elephant. He was eventually committed to a lunatic asylum.

Salvador Dali (1904-89)

Trimmed his huge moustache in 1954 because he felt it was picking up signals from space and thus distancing him from mere earthlings. Dali had a variety of odd habits, including sitting in a cold bath painting if the weather was hot, and pouring coffee and hot milk down his chest in the morning because he enjoyed the sensation.

BURIAL

Shah Khan Jahan

This 13th-century Mogul emperor was buried with his hand out of the tomb so that visitors could shake it.

Charles I (1600-49)

Ben Jonson asked Charles for a square foot in Westminster Abbey after his death. The King took him literally and buried him in an upright position.

Jemmy Hirst (1738-1829)

This Rawcliffe farmer had a coffin made with small windows and shelves in it, and left money in his will for it to be carried, accompanied by a piper, fiddler and 12 elderly virgins to his grave. In the event, however, the vicar objected to the fiddle and only two virgins could be found, who were accompanied by ten widows to make up the numbers.

Hannah Beswick

When Beswick died in Manchester in 1758, she made arrangements for her body to be preserved for a hundred years as she was afraid that she might not be truly dead when she appeared to be. This was a fairly common phobia of the 18th century, and there are reasons to suppose one of Hannah's brothers came out of a trance just as his coffin lid was being screwed down. Hannah, left her doctor £25,000 to visit her corpse regularly to ensure she hadn't revived. He cut down on travelling time by keeping it in his own house. He kept it inside a grandfather clock for the next 45 years, looking inside the clock at regular intervals for signs of life, but then died himself. The 'Manchester Mummy' (as Hannah was now called) was eventually transferred to the Museum of Natural History until 1868, when Hannah was finally put under the ground.

Niccolo Paganini (1782-1840)

This egotistical violinist was so flamboyant in his style of play – bouncing the bow over the strings, breaking strings (which he had weakened in advance) to demonstrate how he could still carry on without them, and making animal squeals and grunts – that many people felt he was possessed by the devil. So much so, that when he died, French church authorities refused to bury him. His coffin lay in a cellar for five years before it was finally accepted for burial in his home town of Parma in Italy.

Henry Trigg

The 18th-century grocer was so afraid of his body being stolen from a graveyard (a common practice of the time) that he made a will stating that he wanted his remains stored in his barn. The will stated that if his brother didn't abide by this request, he would be disinherited. The coffin was eventually wedged into the barn roof in 1724 but a century later the wood started to rot so the coffin was replaced with a new one and Henry's remains taken out. The coffin, however, can still be seen in the barn roof – which would rather seem to defeat the purpose.

Sir Thomas Barrett-Leonard (1857-1918)

This Essex squire gave his pets full-scale funerals. He led the cortèges dressed in a long white robe and read prayers as their coffins were lowered into their graves.

Aimee McPherson (1890-1944)

Daughter of a Methodist father and Salvation Army mother who made the world her stage both in life and beyond it. Her first ambition was to be an actress but when this shocked her parents, she opted to become an evangelist instead, exchanging the stage for the pulpit. She insisted on being buried with a phone in her coffin so that she could send messages back from 'the other side'. After seven years of silence, however, it was disconnected.

Lionel Barrymore (1878-1954)

As his exhibitionistic father, Maurice, an actor, was being buried, the coffin chord became snagged as it was going into the ground and the coffin had to be raised again to free it. 'How like father,' Lionel remarked drily, 'a curtain call.'

Margaret Thompson

Someone who truly 'snuffed it', Margaret was a 19th-century dowager who arranged for her coffin to be filled with snuff handkerchiefs. Her pallbearers were to take snuff before they carried her coffin out of the church, six girls were to walk behind the hearse with boxes of snuff, as was the priest. Her servants were to throw some more of it towards the mourners and her body was to be covered with Scotch snuff instead of flowers.

Harry Bagshaw

In 1927, this Derbyshire cricketer was buried in his umpire's coat, and with a cricket ball in his hand.

Mike Meaney

For an endurance test, this Irishman allowed himself to be buried alive in a closed casket under a pub in London in 1968 for 61 days.

Sandra West

The Beverly Hills society lady who died in 1977 specified in her will that she be buried 'next to my husband in my lace nightgown in my Ferrari, with the seat slanted comfortably'. Two months later, after some legal wrangling, the said Ferrari was duly lowered into a gigantic plot containing two truck loads of concrete.

CHILDHOOD

Harry Houdini (1874-1926)

By the age of seven, Houdini was able to suspend himself upside down from a rope and pick pins from the floor with his eyelashes.

Albert Einstein (1879-1959)

The first sentence the scientist ever spoke is alleged to have been 'The soup is too hot'. He was 5 years old. His mother was amazed because he had never said anything beforehand, not even a word. Asked why he hadn't spoken until then, he replied, 'Because I didn't see any need to.' He was so quiet that for a time his parents feared he might even have been retarded.

Benito Mussolini (1883-1945)

'Il Duce', the dictator of Italy, was expelled from school for stabbing a fellow scholar in the buttocks.

Vita Sackville-West (1892-1962)

The author and garden designer used to stuff other children's noses with putty when she was young.

Groucho Marx (1895-1977)

He made his first public appearance as a boy soprano in church, being dismissed eventually for puncturing an organ bellows with a hatpin. He entered vaudeville originally as a female impersonator.

John Betjeman (1906-84)

When he was a small boy, he used to lie on the side of the road pretending to be dead so that passing motorists would stop to see what the matter was. He continued the practice into his adulthood, even as a teacher, much to the delight of the children in his care, who placed bets among themselves as to which vehicles would stop.

Charles Bukowski (1920-94)

The father of the controversial poet/novelist was so punctilious that when Bukowski was a child he had to mow the lawn in front of his California home as if it was a billiard table. If even one blade of grass was left sticking up amongst the others, he was beaten to a frazzle with a razor strop that the old man kept in his bathroom.

Jack Nicholson (1937-)

He grew up under the impression that his mother (who gave birth to him out of wedlock) was his elder sister and his grandmother his mother. His mother's sisters also posed as his sisters. He was 37 before he learned the truth.

Jim Morrison (1943-71)

If he was late for school in youth, his excuse was usually that he had been held up by bandits or else kidnapped by gypsies. He walked out of a classroom one day explaining to his teacher that he was due to be operated on later that day for a brain tumour.

Morrison once tied one end of a piece of string round his ear and put the other end in his mouth. If anybody commented, he said he had a tiny bucket hanging down his throat to collect saliva for medical tests.

COLLECTORS

Richard Heber

Born in Cheshire in 1774, bibliomane Heber was known to have travelled up to 500 miles to procure a title that interested him. He didn't just buy one book at a time, he kept three copies of every book he owned: one for his own use, one for exhibiting and a third for lending. He filled two houses in London with books as well as his family home and went on to fill warehouses in Paris, Antwerp, Ghent and Brussels.

Sir Ashton Lever

The 18th-century squire amassed various collections over his lifetime. He began by collecting birds and had acquired over 5000 when, in 1760, he abandoned his collection to turn his attention to fossil hunting. He tried to exhibit his entire collection in the Leverian Museum in Leicester Square but Londoners were so uninterested that the museum was closed down and the contents sold off in a lottery. This was won by a Mr Parkinson who found himself the proud owner of a vast collection including birds, fossils, weaponry, coral, monkeys, marbles and 'an elephant and zebra, which, when alive, belonged to Her Majesty'.

Prince Christian

This quixotic son-in-law of Queen Victoria lost an eye while hunting one day. Instead of being depressed about having to wear a glass one, he took to his new situation with relish. He ordered over half a dozen different eyes and often took them out to clean them when in company, to the shock of those present. His ocular range came in a variety of colours, including a bloodshot one which he wore whenever he had a cold.

Enrico Caruso (1873-1921)

An Italian operatic tenor who had such a passion for collecting postcards that he used to forward them to himself at his next hotel destination when he was on tour.

29

Maurice Baring (1874-1945)

This wacky English novelist didn't collect books so much as pages of books. In other words if he saw an interesting paragraph or page he ripped it out and filed it. Every time he moved house he left the books he had drawn his collection from behind him, which must have frustrated the new occupants when they got to the missing pages.

Adolf Hitler (1889-1945)

Was fascinated by Greta Garbo and even had his own private print of every film she ever made.

Charles Kay Ogden (1889-1957)

British linguist who was an obsessive collector of all sorts of things including music boxes, shoes, bibles and masks. The masks had a practical purpose: when he was being interviewed he would put one on and urge the interviewer to do so too in an attempt to keep the conversation based on logic without being influenced by personality.

Gore Vidal (1925-)

The prolific American writer is also a bibliophile who only buys houses, so he says, for the sole purpose of having somewhere to store all his books. One of his houses had 42 sofas on which you could sit to read them.

Frank Johnson

This avid string collector from Minnesota retired from collecting in 1971, but not before he had amassed more than five tons of it. He had always found it impossible to resist, be it in the form of shoelaces, pieces of rope or the cords of window sashes, and each day of his life up until then he had gone in search of such items, carrying a leather case with him to store the day's catch – which usually amounted to about ten yards.

Joseph Bowman

Californian workman who was arrested in 1990 for stealing nine tons of bricks from building sites. When police raided his house they found he had a collection of 1327 bricks buried in his back garden in a hole that measured 600 square feet. It took a forklift truck 14 hours to dig them up. The net value was around $3000.

Jose Aubrizo

This Madrid policeman was so fond of teddy bears he took to stealing them. He was arrested in 1993 when 1000 stolen bears were discovered in his house. He was subsequently sent to a mental institution to have his addiction treated.

Jerry Gustav Hasford

This 20th-century author of the novel *The Short Timers* (upon which the Stanley Kubrick movie *Full*

Metal Jacket was based) was once pounced upon by Californian police who had a warrant to search his house for 87 overdue library books. After examining some storage units they found no less than 10,000 books belonging to libraries from England and Australia as well as the U.S.

COMPOSERS

Abbé Debaigne

Music master at the court of Louis XI who created melodies from swine. He chose 12 pigs according to the timbre of their squeal and lined them up in note order. He then made a keyboard which had the relevant keys connected to sharp wires that prodded the pigs and made them squeal as the keys were pressed.

Antonio Vivaldi (1678-1741)

The Italian composer and violinist could compose a concerto in all its parts faster than his copyist could copy it.

Johann Sebastian Bach (1685-1750)

Once wrote an operetta about coffee.

Franz Haydn (1737-1806)

The wife of the composer, Anna Maria Keller, had little respect for his compositions, using them as bin-liners and even curlpapers for her hair.

Wolfgang Amadeus Mozart (1756-91)

At the mere age of two, the child prodigy was able to identify a pig's grunt as being in G-sharp. Mozart composed minuets at five and a year later was able to play the violin and harpsichord. He wrote his first symphony when he was eight.

Ludwig van Beethoven (1770-1827)

After he went deaf he used to put sticks on his piano and bite them, claiming they helped him to hear the melodies being played.

Gioacchino Rossini (1792-1868)

Rossini was so egotistical about his achievements that when writing to his mother he addressed his letters to 'The mother of the great composer'. He once claimed he could put a laundry list to music.

Frederic Chopin (1810-49)

As a child he slept with wooden wedges between his fingers in order to extend their span. Later in life, he only shaved one side of his face for his recitals, as he knew that was all that would be seen.

Richard Wagner (1813-83)

Used to work in an incredibly hot room filled with roses and dressed in a silk dressing gown. He was hypersensitive to criticism and, when invited to listen to his compositions, his friends knew that they had to sing his praises or be violently threatened. He was so anti-semitic, he conducted the music of Mendelssohn only while wearing gloves. When he was finished he flung them on the floor of the concert hall, leaving them to be removed by the cleaners.

Erik Satie (1866-1925)

This rebellious French minimalist composer, a key influence on Debussy and Ravel, enjoyed giving rather strange names to his musical works: Chilled Pieces, Drivelling Preludes (for a Dog), Dried Up Embryos. As well as entertaining himself, the titles helped wind up the music critics he loathed. His works would often offered bizarre instructions for the performer: 'I forbid anyone to read the text aloud during the musical performance. Failure to obey my instruction will provoke my just indignation against anyone so presumptuous.' On another work he commented 'To play this motif 840 times in succession, it would be advisable to prepare oneself beforehand, in the deepest silence, by serious immobilities.' He didn't start composing until he was in his 40s and in later years he became a recluse in an apartment in Arcueil to which he would admit nobody. When he died they found in his wardrobe 84 identical handkerchiefs, along with 12 identical velvet suits and dozens of umbrellas. Amongst all the other oddities of his life, it is worth mentioning that he also tried to found his own church.

Maurice Ravel (1875-1937)

The French composer once wrote a piano piece for a one-armed man.

John Cage (1912-)

This American composer was responsible for a piece of music entitled '4 minutes and 33 seconds'. It consists entirely of silence.

CON MEN

George Psalmanazar (1679-1763)

A Frenchman who arrived in London in 1703 claiming to be from Formosa (now Taiwan), intent on persuading British authorities to allow him teach Formosan at Oxford. This he did, making it all up. (Even his name is now deemed to be pseudonymous.) A few years later he wrote a book called *The Historical and Geographical Description of Formosa* claiming that Formosans ate the flesh of legally executed criminals, and each year offered God 18,000 hearts cut from native boys as a sacrifice.

William Randolph Hearst (1863-1951)

Hearst, on whose career *Citizen Kane* was based, was born into an incredibly wealthy Californian family. He was fascinated by the press and used his fortune to build an enormous journalistic empire in the United States. He would use any tactic to increase circulation and, like some of today's press barons, sacrificed truth for the sake of sensationalism. He used his papers to incite public feeling against the Spanish in the Cuban conflict, and later campaigned against Mexico. He accompanied a photograph of children with their hands in the air walking down a beach with a caption to the effect that they were being pushed into the water to be shot by soldiers. In fact it was a holiday snapshot of children playing and waving at the camera. On another occasion, a picture of 'hunger marchers storming Buckingham Palace' was in reality an old picture of crowds gathering at the palace to hear news of King George V's illness. Hearst never baulked at apologising; he knew that an apology in tiny print would do little to counteract the seeds of doubt and unrest caused by his large headlines.

John Brinkley (1885-1942)

Kansas quack commonly known as 'Goat Gland Brinkley' on account of his claim to be able to rejuvenate men sexually by giving them transplants of the glands or testicles of billy goats – at up to $1500 a go. He did 5000 operations in all.

Henry Miller (1891-1980)

Before he became famous, Miller submitted stories to magazines which had already been published in them years before, merely changing the titles and the names of the characters to avoid detection, which he did successfully.

Charlie Chaplin (1889-1977)

Came third in a Charlie Chaplin lookalike contest held in Monte Carlo.

Graham Greene (1904-91)

Entered a 'Graham Greene Parody' competition in 1949, submitting three entries for his juvenilia under pseudonyms. One of his entries won but the other two weren't placed. The following week Greene wrote to the magazine that ran the competition to say that he was delighted John Smith had won it, but added that he felt John Doakes and William Jones (his other two aliases) also deserved prizes.

Ferdinand Waldo Demara (1921-82)

The self-styled 'Great Imposter' (played by Tony Curtis in the movie of that name) impersonated surgeons, monks, psychology professors and prison officers (among other things) in his chameleon life. He served in the Navy during the 1940s but got out of it by faking his suicide. At a college in Pennsylvania he subsequently 'taught' psychology, having no qualifications in the field whatsoever but having managed to dummy up a CV that fooled the authorities. The FBI finally caught up with him for deserting the Navy and he was sent to prison. On release he practised medicine as an army doctor (again without qualifications), even removing a bullet from near a soldier's heart at one point, and performing a lung re-section on another. He also pulled teeth, removed tonsils and amputated limbs, all with the dexterity of a professional. He learned how to perform these procedures, he claimed, by reading the medical magazine *The Lancet*. He never lost a patient in his life, which meant that the army was sad to say farewell to him after his cover was blown yet again.

His next incarnation was as a prison warden, where he impersonated one Ben Jones at the Texas Department of Correction, but he had to depart this post prematurely after he was 'outed' in a *Life* magazine profile of him recounting his problems with alcoholism. He died in 1982, having lived half a dozen lives in his 60 years. Asked why he did it all he replied jocosely, 'Rascality, pure rascality'.

Quentin Tarantino (1963-)

When the actor and director was looking for film work in his early days, he put down on his CV that he had appeared in Jean Luc-Godard's version of *King Lear*, a lie that wasn't discovered because so little was known about the movie by mainstream directors. (He's still listed in the cast in mid-1990s editions of Leonard Maltin's video guides.)

Walter Danecki

Danecki was a Milwaukee mail sorter who passed himself off as a golf pro during the 1965 Open by faking the application forms. His legitimacy came into question when he shot a 38 over par for the first nine holes, and a 32 over par for the next nine. It was his first and last Open and he went back to his day job afterwards.

Clifford Irving

In 1971, Irving wrote a fake biography of the eccentric recluse Howard Hughes, claiming to be an intimate, though in fact he had never met him. He thought he would get away with it seeing as Hughes was so reluctant to speak to the press about anything, but he was wrong on this count. Hughes exposed the hoax and Irving was sent to prison as a result. While there he gave classes on Creative Writing.

Richard Chamfrey

This gentleman appeared on a French chat-show in 1972 claiming to be the composer Comte de Saint Germain, who was born in 1660.

Alan Conway

Small-time con man who spent many years going round the world pretending to be the film director Stanley Kubrick, getting wined and dined in countries like France, Australia and Switzerland as he made mouthwatering offers to wannabes to put their name in lights. He was finally exposed in 1996.

DEATH

Zeuxis (c.500BC)

Legend has it that this Greek from Heraclea painted so realistically that birds tried to eat a bunch of grapes he painted. He laughed so much at a painting he had done of an ugly woman that he broke a blood vessel and died.

Diogenes of Sinope (412-322BC)

This misanthropic philosopher, most famous as the founder of the Cynics, had an abundance of eccentric ways (see GRUMPS & GROUCHES). He died from eating raw cuttlefish, in an attempt to prove to the world that cooking was unnecessary.

Fabius (275-203BC)

The Roman consul, known as Fabius the Delayer, avoided death in battle but choked to death on a goat hair that was in a plate of milk he was drinking for breakfast one morning.

Attila the Hun (c.406-53)

The marauding King of the Huns, known also as 'the Scourge of God', died on his wedding night due to getting overexcited with his new bride and bursting an artery. His wife was so fearful that the reason for his demise would leak out that she had all the people who made the burial arrangements executed.

Thomas More (1478-1535)

Just as he was about to have his head chopped off for refusing to acknowledge Henry VIII as the leader of the church, he moved his beard out of the way of the guillotine saying, 'This part of me never committed treason'.

Hans Steininger

The 16th-century Austrian had the longest beard in the world, which was ultimately to be his downfall. While he was climbing a staircase he stepped on it by accident and fell down the stairs to his death.

Jean Baptiste Lully (1632-87)

French composer who had a habit of tapping his stick on the floor to keep time. On the 22nd of March 1687 he missed the floor while beating time to 'Te Deum', written to celebrate Louis XIV's recovery from illness, and hit his foot instead. Gangrene set in and he died of the subsequent abscess.

George II (1683-1760)

The King of England died when sitting on a toilet seat.
He broke wind, fell off the seat and smashed his head
on a cabinet as he fell, killing himself with the ferocity
of the blow. Gone with the wind, one might say.

Catherine the Great (1729-96)

The Russian empress died of heart failure on the
toilet after a particularly painful bout of constipation.

Rev. Nigel Hagermore

This Leicestershire Minister used to keep his servants
locked up at night so they wouldn't go out
gallivanting. On New Year's Day in 1746 when he
was on his way to release his domestic staff, one of his
dogs attacked him and he fell into a pond. He
screamed out to the servants for help but, as they were
still locked up, there was nothing they could do for
him and he drowned.

Marie-Antoinette (1755-93)

A lady to the last, she even apologised to her
executioner after accidentally stepping on his toe on
the scaffold moments before she was beheaded.

John Overs

Miserly 18th-century ferry operator from Southwark
who faked his own death for an unusual reason: he

wanted to save money. Imagining he was more loved by his servants than he actually was, he thought his demise would be followed by a collective fast on their part, but as soon as he lay motionless on his bed and convinced them that he had indeed gone to meet his Maker, they decided to celebrate the happy event. Overs listened to the merry-making with increasing disgust and when he could take it no more he leaped up from his bed. One of the revellers got such a shock upon seeing him that he thought he was the devil and struck him a fatal blow to the head with an oar.

Allan Pinkerton (1819-84)

The Scottish-born founder of the famous U.S. Pinkerton Detective Agency, which specialised in catching railway thieves, died merely from taking a stroll: he bit his tongue and gangrene set in as a result.

Gabriele D'Annunzio (1863-1938)

Firebrand poet and politician from Italy's Fascist era who wanted to die by having his body either fired from a cannon into the air or dipped in a vat of acid.

Sherwood Anderson (1876-1941)

This writer died from peritonitis after swallowing a toothpick in an *hors d'oeuvres* sausage.

Jim Morrison (1943-1971)

The iconic lead singer from The Doors used to fantasise about dying in a plane crash, saying, 'It would be a good way to go. I don't want to drift off in my sleep. I want to taste it, hear it, smell it. Death is only going to happen once and I don't want to miss it.'

Jae Nguyen

A woman who sued the Chicago Transit Authority in 1991 after her husband had electrocuted himself while having a pee on the railway track, his urine contacting the rail and sending 600 volts through his body. A Korean emigrant, the unfortunate man had been unable to read the danger signs. She won $1 million in damages.

DELUSIONS OF GRANDEUR

Caligula (AD12-41)

The Roman emperor imagined himself to be the god Jupiter. A belief of the time was that Jupiter caused thunder and lightning, which prompted Caligula to create a machine that produced similar effects. He then bellowed at the sky, 'Destroy me or I'll destroy you'. If anyone denied he was divine they were put to the sword. He also believed he was a sun god married to the moon, and other divinities as well, like Neptune, Hercules, Bacchus and Apollo.

Margaret Lucas

The 17th-century author who went on to become the Duchess of Newcastle was scribbling ferociously from her pre-teens, but cared little for editing, punctuation or spelling. She hated exercise because she felt movement killed her inspiration. She was content to write and not be published until the day she lost faith in an afterlife; at this time she became desperate to see her work on shelves for posterity, but it was so abysmal publishers merely laughed at it. She wrote 14 plays in all, most of them unperformable, awash as they were with witless dialogue, rambling five-page soliloquies, and characters with names like Monsieur Vain-Glorious, Madam Caprisia and Sir Peachable Studious. The Duchess was sometimes inspired in the middle of the night, and would call out to her secretary, 'I conceive! I conceive!' Her servant would then have to rise from his bed and transcribe her thoughts onto a notepad.

Her non-writing habits were equally unusual. When she met people in the street she bowed low to the ground and started talking manically to them, her head shaking wildly as she ranted on about subjects such as what substance the moon was made of or whether snails had teeth. She held some strange beliefs, thinking cancer was caused by too much salt, snow was nothing but curdled water and all winds came from Lapland.

She finally attained literary success towards the end of her life when she wrote a biography of her husband the Duke of Newcastle, but she is primarily remembered today for the singular direness of her plays and poems – and her belief in her own genius.

Timothy Dexter

Born in 1747 to a poor family in Massachusetts, Dexter had something of a messianic complex. An entrepreneur of note, after he made his fortune from speculating with foreign currency, he decided to call himself 'Lord Timothy' and establish his own court. His courtiers included his nagging wife and alcoholic son as well as a poet laureate and a tall idiot he called The Dwarf. The poet he dressed in a cocked hat and silver-buckled shoes. As befitted a lord, he built a lavish mansion within which to house these luminaries. He also wrote a book about his life which sold well, despite containing no punctuation whatsoever, and having its capital letters invariably inserted in the wrong places. On the last page of the book he provided a list of forms of punctuation and invited the reader to insert them into the main text as they wished. The book's main thesis was that America needed an emperor, and Timothy was only too willing to fill the role. America, however, didn't take him up on his offer.

Robert Coates

Undisputedly one of the worst actors in British theatrical history, Coates specialised in wearing costumes totally at variance with the characters he played. For Romeo, for instance, he donned a top hat and a blue silk coat, and for Lothario a silk stole and a hat with ostrich feather plumes. He frequently forgot lines or added to them as he saw fit, and sometimes even waved to members of the audience in the middle of his performances. He was often booed on stage, and once drew a sword on a heckler who failed to appreciate his genius. During one performance of *Romeo and Juliet* in 1811, he delivered the line, 'Oh let me hence: I stand on sudden haste', an obvious exit cue, but instead of leaving the stage he fell on all fours and started scrambling round the floor. To cries of consternation from the director he replied, 'I can't leave until I find my knee buckle!' The audience erupted into laughter. Indeed, it was the possibility of such moments of wonderful nonsense that brought them to his performances in their droves.

Sometimes, if his death scene got an enthusiastic response from the audience, he resurrected himself momentarily to take bows from them, and then 'died' again. Some people were even known to cry out 'Die! Die!' to him when he continued to make a meal out of his demise on stage.

William McGonagall (1825-1902)

Generally regarded as the worst poet Scotland ever produced, and still revered for that, McGonagall started his professional career as an actor, drawing some praiseworthy notices for his performance as Macbeth at the Theatre Royal ... at least until the night he was enjoying the performance so much he refused to lie down and die and Macduff had to use real physical force to get him on the ground.

He brought equal enthusiasm to his poetry, which was uniformly abysmal. Proving the truth of F. Scott Fitzgerald's dictum that all bad writers are in love with the epic, he chose big themes upon which to unleash his pen and was dubbed the 'Scottish Homer' after his production of *The Epigoniad*. He believed in his ability so much he even sought a rendezvous with Queen Victoria, walking all the way from his native Dundee to Balmoral so that he could read some of his verse to her. The Queen wisely declined the offer but William wasn't to be deterred and gave spirited readings of his work to all and sundry, most of whom came to them merely out of a sense of curiosity. He spouted on, blissfully oblivious to the taunts and jeers of his audience, continuing undaunted even when pelted with rotten fruit.

Only Shakespeare, he felt, was superior to him as he blazed on with his glorified doggerel. Fame eluded him, alas, and he died in a pauper's grave. Incidentally, the only writing for which had ever been paid was a rhyme to promote Sunlight Soap.

Amanda McKittrick Ros (1860-1939)

A strong contender for the Worst Writer of All Time
Award, Amanda, from County Down in Ireland, had a
huge faith in her own talents. She began writing at a
young age, showing a pronounced penchant for
naming the characters in her work alliteratively. Over
the next few decades she would create Osbert Otwell,
Irene Iddesleiah, Barney Blocter, Goliath Ginbottle,
Bishop Barelegs. She also evinced a strong regard for
naming people after foods, and in one of her books,
Helen Huddleston, we meet the likes of Lilly Lentil,
Madame Pear, Mrs Strawberry, Peter Plum and
Christopher Currant.

Her style of writing ranged from breathy rhetoric to
quasi-Biblical mumbo-jumbo and people bought her
books often from a perverse excitement to see exactly
how bad she could be. The Oxford Amanda Ros
Society was founded in her honour and here the
literati came to read her works and chortle merrily
over their spectacular ghastliness.

Amanda, meanwhile, stayed blithely indifferent to
her literary failings. In fact if she drew negative reviews
from the critics, as she inevitably did, she remained
defiant in her belief that they hadn't yet Seen The
Light. She brazenly claimed to have received
commendations from all over the world, including
royalty. She replied to her detractors with volleys of
abuse, calling them 'evil-minded snapshots of spleen'
and 'clay crabs of corruption'.

In 1917, due to financial constraints, she had to

convert the ground floor of her house into a shop, which she rented out. The man who took out the lease on it kept it open on Sundays, which flew in the face of her religious principles, so she did everything in her power to keep customers out of it, including posting a banner on the window which read: 'All Desecrators of the Sabbath Shall Be Punished'. (Considering the desecrator in question was giving her money every week for the purpose makes her campaign even more hilarious.)

Amanda contemplated applying for the Nobel Prize for Literature in 1930 but mercifully changed her mind at the last minute. When she died aged 78, the world still hadn't cottoned on to her genius.

Florence Jenkins

This wealthy socialite born in Pennsylvania in 1868 believed she was God's gift to music even though she was totally tone deaf. Her money made it possible for her to organise private recitals at the Ritz-Carlton Hotel in New York, accompanied by her personal pianist. She dressed lavishly for such recitals, bedecked with silk and tinsel like a female (albeit tone deaf) version of Liberace. So many people attended that it was usually standing room only, but their motive was only incredulity at her insane self-belief. She had an accident in a taxi in 1943 which, she claimed, actually improved her singing, enabling her to reach a higher F than ever before. In gratitude she sent the driver a box of cigars.

Newsweek commented: 'In high notes, Mrs Jenkins sounds as if she was afflicted with low, nagging backache.' Such criticism ran off her like water off a duck's back and she continued to perform, bedecked with feathers and throwing rosebuds at her audiences. They crowded in to see this spectacle. Even the Great Caruso turned up to pay his respects one night. He left the auditorium feeling chuffed: his throne was secure for a little while yet.

Charles Clark

This Essex farmer-cum-writer of the 19th century was a bibliophile and filled his house with rare tomes, many of which he reprinted on his own private printing press. He printed his own poems as well, using a variety of pseudonyms like Doggerel Drydog, Malthus Merryfellow, Professor Plypen and Clement Clodpole. He had a marked preference for alliteration, as evinced by many of his booklets (e.g. 'Metrical Mirth about Marriageable Misses', 'The Modern Mode in Matters Matrimonial'). In fact he once wrote a broadside to the *Chelmsford Chronicle*, the title of which consisted of one long alliterative sentence containing 75 words that began with the letter 'p'. He eventually gave up both farming and alliterating, living out his last years as a total hermit in a house where the books were so plentiful they teemed out of every room, clogged staircases and passages and even acted as curtains on his windows, blocking out the tiny amount of light that tried to seep through.

DISLIKES

Percy Bysshe Shelley (1792-1822)

The poet abhorred cats so much he once tied one to a kite in a thunderstorm to electrocute it.

Robert Schumann (1810-56)

The composer hated metal and was particularly averse to touching keys.

Johannes Brahms (1833-97)

The composer loathed cats and used to attempt to shoot them with a bow and arrow out of his window.

Henry Ford (1863-1947)

The car designer had a lifelong dislike of cows after growing up on a farm, despising their docile behaviour. As a result, he encouraged scientists at his laboratories to find substitutes for dairy products so that they would become unnecessary.

Sir Tatton Sykes (1826-1913)

The eccentric Victorian squire hated flowers and took a stick out when walking to knock them down. When he inherited his father's estate he ordered his gardeners to plough it and get rid of all the flowers, instructing them 'If you wish to grow flowers, grow cauliflowers.'

Groucho Marx (1895-1977)

Hated public displays of affection so much that he refused to speak to his daughter Melinda for a year after he saw her kissing her husband on the lips in front of a crowd of people.

Alfred Hitchcock (1899-1980)

The director loved the sight of 'jolly' blood, but was repulsed by the sight of an egg yolk breaking.

John Betjeman (1906-84)

The poet always travelled in smoking compartments even though he wasn't a smoker ... because it was the only way he could be assured he wouldn't be confronted with children.

Robert Maxwell (1923-91)

Hated people smoking in his offices so much that one day when he saw a man lighting up he said 'You're sacked!', handing him a month's wages to ease him on his journey. A few hours later somebody told him the man was only a visitor to the firm.

Bernard Hinault (1954-)

The five-times winner of the Tour de France hates to be touched and has been known to slap children who have done this while asking for his autograph.

Barbara Hutton

The American heiress and ex-wife of Cary Grant divorced Alexis Mdivani on May 13 1935 with the words, 'I shall never marry again'. The following day she married Count Hauwitz-Reventlow.

William Callender

Quirky Londoner who divorced his wife Elsie in 1956 but stayed living with her thereafter anyway. The pair of them had a silent relationship, broken only on Saturday nights between 7 and 9 during their weekly game of Scrabble.

Germaine Greer (1939-)

Divorced Paul de Feu, London's first nude centrefold in *Cosmopolitan* because, after getting up before her one day, he woke her up to get him his breakfast. The marriage lasted three weeks – or, as she puts it herself, three weekends.

Walter Davis

Londoner who divorced his wife Ethel in 1975 and joined a marriage agency to find a new wife. After assimilating all his details, the computer came up with, you've guessed it, Ethel, who had also joined the agency for the same reason. The pair decided there was nothing else for it but to walk up the aisle together again.

Gene Bollard

Bollard and his wife Linda divorced in an unusual fashion in California in 1986, the pair of them freefall parachuting at 120 mph and the divorce lawyer serving the divorce papers on them in mid-air. After a final kiss at 12,000ft, they then dropped out of one another's lives.

Wilhelm Schultz

This disconsolate husband from Stuttgart in Germany divorced his wife Anna in 1994 after she had expressed the desire that her psychiatrist share their bed. Not from any desire for a threesome, she explained, merely so that he could be on hand to analyse Wilhelm's dreams.

DRESS

Henry III (1551-89)

This French king was so eccentric he used to go out walking with a basket full of small dogs hanging round his neck.

Thomas Birch (1705-66)

An 18th-century book keeper at the British Museum who thought the best way to catch fish was to disguise himself as a tree, using his arms as branches and dangling his line outwards, which earned him the nickname Thomas 'The' Birch from locals. Another unusual character trait was a pronounced refusal to wash his clothes. Instead he simply put on clean garments over his dirty ones, sometimes wearing up to five shirts to save himself the task of washing the ones underneath.

Queen Caroline (1768-1821)

This wife of George IV attended a ball in 1814 wearing half a pumpkin on her head, explaining to the Grand Duke that it was the coolest type of coiffure she could think of.

Beau Brummell (1778-1840)

Spent two hours dressing himself every morning to reach the standard of sartorial splendour that befitted such a social butterfly as he was. He dolled himself up to the nines, even to the extent of using champagne froth to polish the soles of his shoes. He wouldn't have a hair out of place and refused to doff his hat to ladies, as was the custom of the time, for fear he wouldn't be able to re-position it at the exact angle he liked. He was so obsessed with his cravat staying in place when he went out for a night that he never turned his head when speaking to people. It was imperative that at dinner parties he was placed beside people he knew, who would understand and not take his rigid stance for hostility.

Brummel was so terrified of picking up dirt on his shoes that when he was going out for an evening he had his servants transport him from his house on a sedan chair, not letting his feet touch the ground until he had arrived at his destination.

Lord Byron (1788-1824)

At Cambridge the 16-stone poet played cricket wearing no less than seven waistcoats in an attempt to lose weight. Unfortunately this failed and he had to resort to a diet of rice and hard biscuits.

Gioacchino Rossini (1792-1868)

The Italian composer best known for *The Barber of Seville* had limited use for a barber himself, being completely bald. Sometimes in winter he was only able to keep his head warm by wearing three wigs at a time.

Jack Mytton (1796-1834)

The Shropshire squire who owned 150 pairs of riding breeches, 1000 hats and over 3000 shirts often abandoned his abundant wardrobe to wade through rivers in skimpy clothing in the depths of winter in pursuit of duck.

Edward Fitzgerald (1809-83)

Poet and scholar famed for his translation of the *Rubaiyat of Omar Khayyam*, Fitzgerald used a tall hat in which to store his books, walking about the place with it tied to his head by means of a hankie.

Franz Lizst (1851-1919)

The composer wore a different coloured cravat every day of the year.

Sir Thomas Barrett-Leonard (1857-1918)

Prosperous Essex squire who dressed like a tramp in his later years, often being given money by visitors to his estate who mistook him for one of the gardeners. One day he was walking across the fields in his grubby apparel when a policeman stopped him and asked him where he had come from. 'Brentwood lunatic asylum!' Sir Thomas replied for a lark, whereupon he was frogmarched to that institution by the long arm of the law.

Henri de Toulouse-Lautrec (1864-1901)

The painter and lithographer who documented Montmartre society in the late 19th century wore a hat at all times, even indoors.

John Christie (1882-1962)

This Eton master and founder of the Glyndebourne Festival Opera played cricket wearing a pink silk vest. When driving his car he usually wrapped an eiderdown round himself. At black tie events he liked to shock by turning up in plimsoll shoes and ill-fitting suits. When he was expected to be dressed casually, on the other hand, he would arrive in a coat and tails. A man who had an obsession with buying in bulk, he owned over 2000 pairs of shoes and 200 shirts. He also had too many socks: when driving along the Bayswater Road in London one day, he suddenly took out a few pairs from an attache case and flung them out the window. He explained to his fellow passenger that it was the easiest way to get rid of them.

Mícháel Mac Liammóir (1899-1978)

Legendary founder member of Dublin's Gate Theatre who liked his toupée so much he even refused to take it off when he was playing a bald man in the TV series *Tolka Row* in the 1960s. He insisted on wearing a bald headpiece over it instead.

Marlene Dietrich (1901-92)

Once owned a gown that was made from the feathers of 300 swans and contained 227,000 hand-sewn beads and a million stitches. Even though she dressed lavishly, she economised on laundry bills, taking her washing to a laundrette in person even when she was mega-famous.

W.H. Auden (1907-73)

Asked if fame would ever change him, the poet replied, 'No, I will never give up my carpet slippers.' When it came his way and he was asked to don a monkey suit for a function, he did so, but wore the slippers as well.

Ian Fleming (1908-64)

Not quite as sartorially impeccable as his main character, James Bond, Fleming wore a favourite blue suit until it practically fell off him. Eventually he wrote a note to his tailor saying, 'Please sew new suit onto these perfectly good buttons.'

Brendan Behan (1923-64)

When J.P. Donleavy complimented Behan on his new suit, he promptly rolled round in a gutter until it looked filthy enough for him to feel comfortable in. Not keen on formal attire, the writer came down to dinner at the Algonquin Hotel one night in an open-necked shirt. The management informed him that ties were essential so he went about remedying the situation. He put on a suit and tie and reappeared at the bar ... only this time he wasn't wearing any shoes or socks.

Andy Warhol (1928-87)

The pioneer of pop art wasn't only fond of reproducing the same image repeatedly, he also used to buy up to a hundred of the same shirts at a go when he went shopping. As a result, people thought he never changed them.

Imelda Marcos (1930-)

At one point of her life this wife of the former president of the Philippines owned 3000 pairs of shoes, 1000 pairs of tights, 500 black bras (one of which was bullet-proof) and 200 girdles.

Woody Allen (1935-)

Didn't only keep his clothes on during a love scene with Helena Bonham Carter in *Mighty Aphrodite,* but his shoes too. 'In case there's a fire,' he explained to her afterwards.

Charlie Bray

Bray is currently the world conker champion (he has even been known to challenge a squirrel to a game) and dresses accordingly: with conkers all over his playing hat, his trousers and shoes. He even wears a bow tie made from them.

DRINK

Richard Brinsley Sheridan (1751-1816)

This Irish author was an inveterate tippler, he would drink eau-de-cologne if there was nothing else available. When told by his doctor that his excessive drinking would destroy the lining of his stomach, Sheridan replied blithely, 'Well then, my stomach must simply learn to digest it in its waistcoat.'

Richard Porson (1759-1808)

Regius Professor of Greek at Cambridge, a contemporary of Byron, and notorious for his drinking binges, Porson even once ingested paraffin from a lamp to slake his thirst.

Another time he was asked to dine by a colleague and replied, 'Thank you, but I already dined yesterday.' This was probably a blessing for the man concerned as Porson was something of a pest to his interlocutors because of his inability to know when his welcome was worn out. He had an encyclopaedic knowledge of the classics – learning he didn't wear lightly – and he could out-drink and out-talk most of his contemporaries.

Horne Tooke, the radical politician, once invited him to dinner – thinking that as he had not slept for 72 hours he would leave early. This wasn't the case and the following morning, after he had been up all night, Tooke pretended he had an appointment at a coffee house to escape from his guest. Porson decided to accompany him and finally, in desperation, Tooke ran away from his verbose companion, instructing his servants not to let him in the house again 'for a man who can sit up for four successive nights could sit up for forty.'

His drinking sprees eventually took their toll and he would try and disguise his bright red nose with a paper cone.

Edmund Kean (c.1789-1833)

The famous tragic actor once got so drunk that he couldn't perform on stage. He contented himself instead with heckling his understudy from a stage box.

Jack Mytton (1796-1834)

Drank up to six bottles of port a day, working off his hangovers by his many athletic pursuits. Finding himself out of it one day, he helped himself to a bottle of lavender at his barber's instead. When annoyed by an attack of hiccups another drunken night, he set fire to his pyjamas to frighten them away. He dined out the following day, his body encased in bandages like a mummy.

Henri de Toulouse-Lautrec (1864-1901)

A hopeless alcoholic, he would drink anything he could get his hands on at all hours of the day and night. He hollowed out his walking stick so that he could put a glass container inside it, which he filled with absinthe, and carried a nutmeg in his pocket to spice his port. The artist was liable to pass out cold without warning if he had imbibed too much, and sleep for anything from two minutes to two hours. Upon waking, he veered from laughter to tears, either insulting his friends, propositioning women or embarking upon another painting.

W.C. Fields (1879-1946)

Brought a thermos of martini onto film sets with him but pretended to his co-stars that it was pineapple juice. One day it was sabotaged, causing Fields to make the classic remark, 'Somebody's put pineapple juice in my pineapple juice.'

John Barrymore (1882-1942)

His drinking and carousing caused him to disappear during many shoots, causing various directors to tear their hair out as they chased him from bar to bar and boudoir to boudoir. The people who cared about him tried to wean him off it gradually but this became a hopeless task. On a boat trip in 1935 with his daughter she took care to have all alcohol removed from the boat, but he still managed to siphon some from the engine's cooling system.

Spencer Tracy (1900-67)

According to a bellhop at a hotel he frequented, the actor would lock himself in his room, strip naked, sit in the tub and drink whiskey incessantly, not even getting out to perform bodily functions. After a week like this he would clean himself up and check out with his suitcase full of empty whiskey bottles and go back to whatever movie set he was working on.

Dylan Thomas (1914-53)

The Welsh poet was given to crawling round floors on his hands and knees when he had one too many (which was most of the time), barking loudly like a wild dog and occasionally snapping at the heels of people sitting at nearby tables.

Montgomery Clift (1920-66)

Clift was so drugged up with booze and painkillers during the filming of *Raintree County* that director Edward Dmytryk had to strap him into a carriage for one scene because he couldn't sit upright. His drinking meant he was unemployable for much of his career, partly due to a decreased ability to remember lines as a result of it.

Richard Burton (1925-84)

Once on stage during a rehearsal of *Henry IV*, Burton felt the call of nature, having drunk 18 half bottles of pale ale, but, as he was dressed in chain-mail armour, director Anthony Quayle was loath to allow him go to the bathroom. So Burton urinated through his costume, leaving a large pool on the stage, and then continued with his lines.

Louis Calhern

This character actor of the 1930s drank so fiercely that, when he appeared in a play on Broadway, the producers locked him in a room on the fourth floor of the Actor's Club to keep him off the sauce. When they were gone, however, he looked out the window and spotted a waiter on the street below. He floated a $20 bill down to him with the plea that he bring a straw and a bottle of whiskey to his room. When the waiter arrived, Calhern told him to put one end of the straw through the keyhole and the other end in the bottle. The producers arrived back to find him sozzled but there was no evidence of any alcohol having been consumed.

Richard Harris (1932-)

This actor was a notorious boozer and often ended up in hospitals or jails due to his drinking binges. Once, mad for a drink, he threw stones up at the window of a house he happened to be passing. The woman inside took pity on him and he ended up staying with her for four days.

Stephen King (1947-)

The author was addicted to alcohol for much of his life, going out each night to get 'as hammered as I could'. The following day he would be hungover until about 2 p.m and would start drinking heavily again in the evening, which meant that his wife could only speak to him for three hours a day. He was afraid to give it up for fear his creativity would disappear.

DRUGS

William Shakespeare (1564-1616)

Recent research indicates the great bard could have been high on dope when he wrote his plays, as scientists have discovered clay pipes at his Stratford home which contain traces of cannabis.

Queen Victoria (1819-1901)

Although few could imagine the normally staid queen getting stoned, she used marijuana to relieve menstrual pains.

Antonin Artaud (1896-1948)

The French playwright, actor, director and theorist of the Surrealist movement, who had a profound influence on post-war theatre, was addicted to both opium and heroin. He once said, 'If I stop taking drugs, that means death. Only death can cure me of the infernal palliative, from which only a precisely calculated absence, not too long in duration, allows me to be what I am.'

Truman Capote (1924-84)

Addicted to alcohol and pills for most of his life, the author used to spread the latter out in front of him like sweets as he experimented with different combinations for the best hit. After he had taken these cocktails he often suffered from severe hallucinations, causing him to phone friends and implore them to rescue him from ghosts.

Elvis Presley (1935-77)

In his later years he couldn't perform without being tanked up with prescription pills. Sometimes he came off stage without even knowing he'd been on. At one point he actually wanted to buy a drugstore so he would have automatic access to whatever he needed. During the last two years of his life he received more than 19,000 doses of uppers and downers from his doctor.

Syd Barrett (1946-)

This sometime Pink Floyd band member spent much of his life out of his tree on LSD. His over-indulgence in this regard caused him to do some pretty mad things both on and off the stage. He smashed a mandolin over one girlfriend's head, and locked another in a room for three days, shoving a ration of biscuits under the door periodically so she didn't starve. When she was eventually rescued he locked himself in instead and refused to come out for a week.

EATING

Anne Boleyn (1507-36)

The second wife of Henry VIII used to be sick during banquets. A lady-in-waiting would stand by, ready to hold up a sheet to conceal the vomiting queen.

Sir Francis Drake (1540-96)

This British admiral and navigator insisted on violin music being played while he ate.

Voltaire (1694-1778)

The French author and philosopher was said to have consumed up to 50 cups of coffee a day. Informed in his eighties that it was 'slow poison' he replied, 'It must be, because I've been drinking it for 65 years and I'm not dead yet!'

Philip Oldenburger

Seventeenth-century political historian from Germany who was forced to eat one of his polemical pamphlets when the government registered its disapproval of it. He was flogged repeatedly until he had digested every last crumb.

Sir Walter Scott (1771-1832)

Had a salt cellar on his table fashioned from the fourth cervical vertebra of King Charles I. It was stolen by a surgeon during an autopsy of the king and came into the possession of Scott, who used it at his table for 30 years until Queen Victoria demanded its return.

Beau Brummell (1778-1840)

The dandy was not only particular about his sartorial arrangements, but also about his partner's dietary predilections: he once left a woman because he discovered she liked cabbage. He seems to have had an animosity towards vegetables and professed to have only eaten one pea in his life, and no other vegetables at all.

Kitty Fisher

This (in)famous 18th-century prostitute charged the then astronomical 100 guineas per night for her services. Upon receiving only half that amount from Edward, Duke of York one night, she proceeded to take the money, put it into a sandwich and eat it.

Victor Hugo (1802-85)

The most prolific French writer of the 19th century, author of *The Hunchback of Notre Dame*, often ate up to six oranges at a sitting, without bothering to remove the peel.

Menelik II (1844-1913)

This Ethiopian emperor had an unusual hobby: he tended to consume various pages of the Bible when he wasn't feeling well as he felt there were healing properties in the printing materials. He died after being unable to digest the appropriately named Book of Kings.

James Brady (1856-1917)

American railroad magnate who ate so much that, on his own admission, he always started a meal sitting four inches away from the edge of the table and stopped when he felt his stomach rubbing against it. New York restaurateur Charles Rector described him as 'the best 25 customers I ever had'. He breakfasted on eggs, muffins, cornbread, flapjacks, chops, fried potatoes and beefsteak, all of which he washed down with a gallon of orange juice. Elevenses consisted of two or three dozen clams and oysters and at lunch he had more of the same, topped up with boiled lobster, crab, a joint of beef and another gallon of orange juice. At teatime he had a platter of seafood washed down with lemon soda and at dinner he had more oysters and crab as well as two bowls of green turtle soup. This, it should be emphasised, was only the appetiser, the main course consisting of six or seven lobsters, two ducks, a large sirloin steak with assorted vegetables and pastry for dessert. Before going to bed he often wolfed down a full box of chocolates as a nightcap.

With such a diet he was obviously a heart attack waiting to happen but incredibly he lived until he was 61, a post mortem revealing that his stomach was six times the normal size.

J.M. Barrie (1860-1937)

The author of *Peter Pan* ordered Brussels sprouts constantly when he went out to eat but always left them on the plate. When an acquaintance enquired why, he said, 'Because the words sound so lovely'.

Vita Sackville-West (1892-1962)

Always ate outdoors, wearing a fur coat in winter and putting a hot water bottle over her knees to keep herself warm.

Elvis Presley (1935-77)

The iconic singer who became more corpulent as the years went on once travelled 500 miles on his private jet in order to get a peanut butter sandwich he liked.

Andy Kaufman (1949-84)

After a performance at the Carnegie Hall, Kaufman decided to carry on the celebrations and had the 1,500 audience members transported by bus to West 49th Street for a milk and cookies party.

Raymond Dorneaux

French local government officer who broke off his engagement to his fiancée in 1953 when she refused to cook him his favourite dish: pickled calves' heads. His mother had given it to him almost every day since he was six and he found the concept of marriage without it unthinkable, so he stayed with mama.

Jay Gwaltney

Ate an 11-foot birch tree leaf by leaf in 1978 for a dare. It took him 89 hours to digest it totally.

Web Hastings

Nevada man who became addicted not to smoking cigarettes but to eating them. In the early 1990s he ate up to 60 day in a buttered sandwich he sprinkled with mustard and salt.

Ellen Greve

Brisbane-born lady (aka Jasmuheen) who became a multi-millionairess from her book *Living on Light* which posits the theory that you don't need food to survive, only 'prana' or 'God's light'. She claims she hasn't eaten a meal since 1993 and thus believes she's found a solution to the problem of world hunger. Sadly, in the past four years three people have died trying to put her controversial '21 Day Process' into practice.

EXTRAVAGANCE

Virgil (70-19BC)

Spent the current equivalent of £50,000 on the funeral of his pet fly.

Firdausi (940-c.1020)

This Persian poet once paid the equivalent of £1 million for a glass of beer.

Ibrahim the Mad (1616-48)

Solipsistic sultan of the Ottoman Empire who had his beard encased in diamonds and also had his cats shaved and dressed in sable coats.

William Beckford (1760-1844)

English art collector and builder of follies, author of the Gothic novel *Vathek* and friend of Voltaire,

Beckford inherited a vast fortune from his father, who was Lord Mayor of London, which made him one of the wealthiest people in Britain in the 18th century. He had an incredibly lavish lifestyle and was given music lessons by Mozart. When he decided he wanted to go for a ride through a certain wood, he commanded the entire working population of the nearest village to clear a path through it for him. On a visit to Portugal he was underwhelmed by the view from the window of the inn at which he was staying so ordered a flock of sheep to be imported from England to improve the situation.

Architecture was his main hobby and he recruited the assistance of many to build a vast complex of turrets and towers on his estate, including the 276-foot Fonthill Abbey designed by James Wyatt which could be seen from miles around.

Percy Bysshe Shelley (1792-1822)

The Romantic poet used to love sailing paper boats so much (even in adulthood) that if he had no paper handy he used bank notes instead.

Jack Mytton (1796-1834)

An MP who lived a rollercoaster life of thrills and spills. A turbo-charged individual from childhood, no nanny or schoolmaster could ever control him and he was expelled from all the schools he attended. A home tutor employed to try and educate him packed his bags after being beaten to a pulp by Master Mytton.

When his father died, Jack inherited a lump sum of £60,000, and an annual £10,000 in annuities thereafter, all of which he proceeded to spend in record time. He gambled most of it away but didn't ever seem to care about winning. One day, after coming home from a horse meet with a wad of notes, a wind came up and blew them out of his carriage. Jack watched them sail through the air unconcerned and didn't even bother to retrieve them.

However his fortune soon disappeared and he fled to Calais in 1831 to escape his creditors. He returned three years later and was put into a debtor's prison. Here he died of *delirium tremens* at the age of 37, a victim of his excesses.

James Gordon Bennett (1841-1918)

This wacky newspaper magnate once gave a $14,000 tip to a train guard (who immediately resigned from his job to buy a restaurant).

One day he found his favourite Monaco restaurant full. The only way to get a table was to buy it on the spot and evacuate all the diners. This he duly did, whereupon he then sat down and ate seven mutton chops generously topped with gravy. After he had eaten and supped he gave the restaurant back free to the former owner – on condition that he be allowed to drop in any time he wanted for his mutton chops and be assured of getting a table. After a few moments of consideration the man agreed to this request.

Henry Ford (1863-1947)

The self-made American automobile manufacturer once tried to buy the Eiffel Tower, intending to ship it to the U.S., but the French refused. He wasn't generally keen to part with his cash though and often gave gifts of cars to his employees, telling them they had them for life, but just as quickly withdrew them on some flimsy pretext.

Ned Green (1868-1936)

Ned was the unfortunate son of Hetty Green, the notorious 'Witch of Wall Street' (See SKINFLINTS) and he was determined not to live the life she did. He went to the opposite extreme, going through over $3 million a year, which was heavy spending at that time, even for a man of his means.

He collected cars, yachts, diamond-encrusted chastity belts and (his favourite) whale penises. The largest of the latter measured an amazing 14 feet.

Thomas Beecham (1879-1961)

The Lancashire conductor and impresario, noted for his candid views on the musical world, was out walking one day when he felt himself sweating. He hailed a taxi and asked the driver to take his coat from him. He then instructed him to follow him in the taxi in case the weather turned cold and he needed the coat again.

Cecil B. De Mille (1881-1959)

Producer and director known for the grandeur of his films, De Mille went to extraordinary lengths to achieve the effects he wanted. In order to help Moses part the waves in *The Ten Commandments,* he had built a water tank so large that the brick wall between RKO Studios and Paramount had to be pulled down to accommodate it. It held 360,000 gallons of water which was poured from 15 manually controlled valves over a concrete ramp 32 feet high and 80 feet long. When he was making the original *Cleopatra*, De Mille sent his art director to Egypt (at a cost of $1,000,000) to find out what colour pyramids were. Fine ... if it wasn't for the fact that the film was shot in black and white.

Maharajah of Gwalior (1886-1925)

Indian prince whose capricious rule in the early 1900s caused many tongues to wag. He was something of a spendthrift to say the least, his *pièce de resistance* being a railway which linked the kitchen of his mansion to the banqueting hall. The electrical model engine ran on 250 feet of track, making designated stops to allow diners to pick and choose from the Maharajah's juicy smorgasbord. The setting was also lavish: hanging above all of the guests was a gigantic chandelier. It was so enormous and heavy that he first had to have the strength of the roof tested to ensure it wouldn't fall down on top of all of them: he did this by having an elephant lowered onto it.

The Maharajah was also something of a sentimentalist and when his mother died he built a marble statue in her memory. This was no ordinary statue, mind. In fact each day he had his servants wash and dress it, and even shower it with perfumes and jewellery. Food was left at its feet (usually uneaten, sadly) and its face was fanned on hot days to ensure the old dear wouldn't overheat.

Adolph Menjou (1890-1963)

During the periods when he was unemployed, the actor used to have his chauffeur drive him to the social security office to collect his welfare cheque in his Rolls Royce.

Bhupinder Singh (1891-1938)

This Indian prince set new standards of extravagance in the early 1900s. He ordered shirts by the gross, and spent £30,000 a year on underpants, most of which he threw away after wearing them once. He also had 130 cars. When he visited London in 1925 he took over all 25 suites on the fifth floor of the Savoy. He brought 200 items of luggage with him, and a travelling staff of 50. Three thousand fresh roses were brought to his rooms each day, and neither did he stint on food, wolfing down approximately 50 pounds of it daily. He ordered quail one day but it wasn't on the menu so he had it flown in from Egypt.

Aristotle Onassis (1906-75)

The electrical power that was used for his yacht could have lit a city of 10,000 people. Whenever he organised banquets on his ships he had the cooks double up on everything that was on the menu. Thus there were two effective banquets laid out: one on deck if the day was fine and the other down below if it wasn't. The uneaten food was thrown away.

Elvis Presley (1935-77)

The singer gave away presents of cars to total strangers if he ran into them at garages, forlornly viewing automobiles they could never expect to be able to afford.

FEAR

Queen Christina (1626-89)

Swedish queen who was so frightened of fleas she had a cannon built to blast them to eternity. Its barrel was only four inches wide and the cannonballs smaller than marbles.

Samuel Johnson (1709-84)

The writer and lexicographer feared insanity so much

that, if he felt as though he was bordering on the brink of madness, he had his wife Tetty lock him up in his room until he had calmed down.

Catherine the Great (1729-96)

The Empress of Russia was so terrified that the world would learn she had dandruff, she imprisoned her hairdresser in an iron cage for three years to stop her blabbing.

Richard Kirwan (1733-1812)

Irish linguist who was so afraid of flies he paid his servants an extra stipend for each one they delivered dead to his door in Dublin's Parnell Square.

Hans Christian Anderson (1805-1875)

This author had many fears: fear of drowning, fear of being murdered, fear of dogs, fear of poverty and even fear of losing his passport. Before going to sleep at night he checked his bedside candle up to 20 times to make sure it was extinguished. His fear of fire was so intense that he brought a piece of rope with him any-time he was staying in an inn so that he could lower himself from a window with it if one started. He was so petrified about being buried alive that he used to leave a note beside his bed each night to be read by anyone finding him comatose. It said, 'I only appear to be dead. I am in suspended animation. Cut one of my arteries before sealing my coffin.'

Edward Lear (1812-1888)

The author and artist was terrified of horses and dogs.

Fyodor Dostoevsky (1821-81)

The Russian author was so terrified of being buried alive that whenever he was sleeping away from home he left a note beside his bed specifying that if he appeared to be dead he wasn't to be buried until exhaustive tests were performed on him.

Peter Ilyich Tchaikovsky (1840-93)

Had such a fear that his head would roll off his shoulders while he was conducting that he held his chin with his left hand during concerts. Such a phobia lasted his whole life long.

Alexander Graham Bell (1847-1922)

This Scottish educationist and inventor of the telephone kept his windows covered at night because he was afraid of the rays of the moon.

Sir Herbert Draper Beerbohm Tree (1853-1917)

The witty and eccentric thespian travelled only once in a motorcar and was so terrified by it he spent most of the journey on the floor peeping out the window with his hands over his eyes

Sigmund Freud (1865-1939)

The king of solving other people's fears had an unusual phobia of his own: a fear of trains.

P.G. Wodehouse (1881-1975)

When visiting his adopted daughter Leonora at her school outside London he often hid in the bushes outside the premises because he was afraid of her headmistress. He would lie there with a handkerchief on his head knotted at the four sides to protect himself from the sun, causing her friends huge fits of giggles when they spotted him.

Bela Lugosi (1882-1956)

Famed for drinking blood in his role as Dracula, Lugosi was actually prone to fainting spells at the sight of his own blood.

Adolf Hitler (1889-1945)

He had a terror that his father's mother had had an affair with a Jew, resulting in the birth of his father Alois. This would have made him partly Jewish himself. Such suspicions fuelled his antisemitism.

Katharine Hepburn (1907-)

The actress had such a phobia about germs she used to go around film sets sniffing the hair of her co-stars to make sure it was clean.

Elvis Presley (1935-77)

Girlfriends had to wait for the singer to fall asleep first every night as he hated being awake alone in the dark. This was one reason he lived like a nocturnal animal, usually only going to bed when the sun came up.

Marvin Gaye (1939-92)

Suffered so much from stagefright that one night he even tried to climb out the window of his dressing room to avoid having to face the public.

John Waters (1946-)

The film director fears electricity so much he thinks he'll die every time he plugs something in. He's also terrified to turn on heaters in case his house blows up.

Sam Snead (1912-)

This American golfer has a terror of losing his hair and sometimes walks on his hands to stop the process, having read somewhere that a blood rush to the head would stimulate his follicles.

FETISHES

Tiberius (42BC-AD37)

This Roman emperor trained little boys to chase him when he went swimming. After they caught up with him they were instructed to get in between his legs and nibble him.

Samuel Pepys (1663-1703)

Used to buy pornographic books, read them at a sitting and masturbate as he did so. He then burned them to destroy the evidence, but noted all his masturbations in his diary using a special symbol.

Charles Waterton (1782-1865)

This quirky squire had a fantasy about having his toe sucked by a vampire bat.

Fyodor Dostoevsky (1821-81)

The Russian novelist had a foot fetish, which caused him to remark to his wife Anna Smitkina once: 'I go down on my knees before you and I kiss your dear feet a countless number of times – I imagine this every minute'.

Algernon Swinburne (1837-1909)

The author became hooked on flagellation when he was at Eton and subsequently graduated (if that's the word) to an interest in copulating with animals. One day he dressed a monkey up in women's clothes and attempted to make love to it, but the monkey didn't share his enthusiasm and attacked him. Swinburne wasn't impressed and dined that night on grilled monkey.

Havelock Ellis (1859-1939)

The physician who published the then controversial *Psychology of Sex* had a fetish for watching women urinate. The fascination began at the age of 12 at London Zoo when he watched his mother doing it. Late in his life he used to watch his lover, Francoise, urinate. He enjoyed watching her pee in the rain as they walked along together.

André Gide (1869-1951)

Great French author who was attracted to little boys, particularly crippled or deformed ones. When he was with a prostitute he could only become aroused by pretending to himself that she was actually her little brother.

Marcel Proust (1871-1922)

The French author became sexually excited by playing a game which involved putting two starving rats in separate cages, then opening the cages and watching them tear one another to pieces. He also enjoyed watching clients of a male brothel being beaten from a private window.

James Joyce (1882-1941)

Liked to be mothered, and even flogged, by his wife Nora until his flesh throbbed. He was also an underwear fetishist and kept a pair of doll's panties with him at all times, putting them on his fingers and 'walking' them across bar counters in Dublin.

Franz Kafka (1883-1924)

Had a fantasy of being sliced apart by a pork butcher's knife, first by somebody else and then by himself, the knife cutting shards out of him as from a piece of wood or a slice of cheese.

Duke Ellington (1889-1974)

The composer and bandleader from Washington was attracted to women with scars.

Adolf Hitler (1889-1945)

Had a penchant for having women both urinating and defecating on him, according to his niece Geli Reubal, with whom he had an affair.

FUSSPOTS

Ivan the Terrible (1530-84)

When he was looking for a wife he vetted over 2000 women. The two main prerequisites were that they be virgins and that they didn't snore in bed.

Jonathan Swift (1667-1745)

When his maid forgot to shut the door after her one day, he had one of his servants follow her on horseback for miles to advise her of her lapse and bring her back to correct it.

Frederick the Great (1688-1740)

This Prussian leader ordered buttons to be sewn on the sleeves of army uniforms to prevent soldiers wiping their noses on them.

Jean Vatel

A chef to Louis XIV who took his job rather seriously, to say the least. When the lobster sauce for Louis' turbot was late arriving one day, he became so distraught at the gastronomic unpunctuality he stabbed himself fatally in the heart with his sword.

Anthony Trollope (1815-82)

The pedantic author wrote seven pages every day. If he finished one of his books before he had reached this tally, he would make it up by starting a new one. Trollope held the belief that nothing could make people truly happy except writing and devoted himself to this craft by having his Irish servant Barney call him religiously at five o'clock every morning with coffee, paying him £5 per annum extra for this added chore. He was at his desk by half past five and would spend the next half hour scanning his previous day's work. He then wrote 250 words every 15 minutes thereafter, keeping a close eye on his watch to make sure he met his word-count.

Andrew Carnegie (1838-1919)

The demanding steel magnate was inspecting a factory he owned one day when he spotted an old employee and started chatting to him. He asked him how many years he had been working there and the man said 'Thirty-nine'. When he asked him how many mistakes he'd made in that time, the man trilled 'Only one'. Carnegie replied, 'Good work, but from now on, please try and be more careful.'

Paul Cezanne (1839-1906)

A thoroughly meticulous artist, he was once painting a portrait of a man that wasn't coming out to his liking. After calling to the studio over a hundred times, the man asked how it was coming along. 'I am not entirely unhappy with your shirt front,' the artist reassured him.

Sir Herbert Draper Beerbohm Tree (1853-1917)

When in a post office, the thespian asked the girl behind the counter if she sold stamps. When she said she did he asked to be shown a card of them. He studied the identical stamps avidly for a few moments before pointing at one of them and saying, 'I'll have that one.'

Prince Cherkassy

This 19th-century Russian royal used to get his gardeners (he had 48 of them) to change the plants in his flowerbeds every day because he hated waking up to the same view two mornings in a row.

Paul Dirac (1902-84)

The English physicist, the father of quantum mechanics, was notoriously literal in his thinking. If you said 'Good morning' to him, he was liable to look up at the sky to make sure you were right before replying. In fact, one night when a dinner companion remarked that it was windy outside, Dirac looked at him in silence for some moments before leaving his seat, going out to the door, looking out, returning to his seat and finally returning to the table to say 'Yes'.

On another occasion, after one of his lectures, a student stood up and said he hadn't understood how Dirac had arrived at a particular conclusion. Dirac looked at the student but didn't say anything. When it became apparent that he wasn't going to say anything the chairman said to him, 'Are you not going to answer the question?' Dirac looked at him and said sternly, 'It wasn't a question: it was a statement.'

Georges Simenon (1903-89)

The creator of Inspector Maigret was so particular about his writing that he saw to it that all his books would have the same length (200 pages) and the same number of chapters (11). He wrote a chapter a day, keeping rigorously to this formula. If it was disrupted for any reason, he merely tossed the chapter aside. He wrote almost 400 novels, 193 in his own name and more than 200 under 18 different pseudonyms. In one year alone he wrote 44 books, an average of almost one a week.

Jack Lemmon (1925-2001)

Had a meeting on the set of his movie *Pffft* solely to discuss whether there should be two or three 'f's' in the title.

Kenneth Williams (1926-88)

For a man who acted in so many films that featured toilet humour, Williams was surprisingly fussy about his own little boys' room and wouldn't invite people to his London flat for fear they would want to use it.

GAMBLERS

John Montagu (1718-92)

Montagu, the 4th Earl of Sandwich, was such a compulsive gambler that he begrudged the amount of time he had to spend away from his card table to eat, so organised pieces of cooked meat to be served between two pieces of bread during his games. The modern sandwich, of course, has been named in his honour.

Lord March (1725-1810)

This Duke of Queensbury was an inveterate gambler. He once made a bet he could send a letter at 50 miles an hour. His trick lay in placing 24 cricket players in a circle and putting the letter inside a ball. The speed at which they passed the ball among themselves ensured they reached his limit effortlessly.

Wolfgang Amadeus Mozart (1756-91)

Once bet Haydn that he could write a piece of music Haydn wouldn't be able to play. Haydn took the bet but found himself flummoxed by the piece Mozart presented him with, which involved the main chords being played at either end of the piano and, infuriatingly, a single note in the middle of the keyboard. Haydn finally admitted it was unplayable, whereupon Mozart sat down, put one hand at either end of the piano and started to play. When he got to the awkward middle note he did what any practically-minded composer would do: used his nose.

Niccolo Paganini (1782-1840)

The flamboyant violinist often had to pawn his violin to pay his gambling debts.

Fyodor Dostoevsky (1821-81)

Was a compulsive gambler – so much so that his wife had to hock her wedding ring at one point to put bread on the table.

John Warne Gates (1855-1911)

This enterprising American millionaire placed outrageous bets for the fun of it, once winning $20,000 on predicting the path of a drop of water on the window of a train during a boring journey.

Neither was he averse to some underhand tactics when it came to relieving fellow gamblers of their cash. One day while dining with wealthy playboy John Drake, the son of the Governor of Iowa, he suggested they both dip their bread into their coffee, with $1000 per fly going to the man whose bread

attracted the most flies afterwards. A bevy of them
buzzed round Gates's slice and he won. What Drake
didn't realise was that Gates had put six lumps of
sugar into his cup before making the bet, which tilted
the odds in his favour.

GROSSNESS

Michelangelo (1475-1564)

The Italian artist was so absorbed in his work that he
went without washing during the four years he was
painting the Sistine chapel.

Giovanni Casanova (1725-98)

One wonders whether women would have been so
susceptible to Casanova's seductive techniques had
they known he used to grow the nail on his little
finger extra long so that he could pick the wax out of
his ears with it.

Frank Buckland (1826-80)

This surgeon and naturalist was a founder member of
the Society for the Acclimatisation of Animals in the
U.K., an organisation devoted to increasing the
nation's food supplies by breeding anything from kan-
garoos to bison. He tried out recipes using not only

kangaroo meat and South East Asian sea slugs but also earwigs, boiled elephant's trunk, roast ostrich and rhinoceros pie. He found broiled porpoise head distasteful, lamenting that it tasted like an oil lamp wick.

Frank's father William was equally strange and his main claim to gastronomic fame was that he had eaten the heart of Louis XIV, which had been plundered from the royal tomb during the French Revolution. 'I have eaten many strange things in my life,' he confessed, 'but never before the heart of a king.'

Joseph Pujol (1857-1945)

This Marseilles baker born in 1857 noticed that when bathing he could contract his stomach muscles, take in water through his backside and then shoot a long jet of it from his bottom. He also discovered he could create a wide variety of sounds when farting, causing him to become known as 'Le Petomane' or 'the mad farter'. He set up a stage act, first in Marseilles and then at Le Moulin Rouge in Paris, that had audiences pouring in in their droves as soon as they got wind of this unusual performance. Not only did he have a range of 'human' farts – girl, bride, boy, workman – his rear end could simulate sounds like thunder, cannon fire and calico being torn. He could even play 'Au Clair de la Lune' with his bum.

He had many imitators, one of whom he sued for using a bellows-like contraption up her *derriere* to produce the same sounds as he did. He himself sometimes performed in a bathing-suit with a hole at the anus so he could prove that his gift was natural.

After a row with the management at Le Moulin Rouge, he set up his own Theatre Pompadour, and his act was still going strong until the early 20th century when his audience dwindled and he returned to baking.

Henri de Toulouse-Lautrec (1864-1901)

Didn't restrict himself to images of suave Parisian cafe society and once drew a caricature of himself vomiting from his bed. In 1900 he posed delightedly for a photographer who snapped him defecating on a beach.

John Christie (1882-1962)

Christie dined frequently with Queen Elizabeth II. He once pulled out his glass eye in her company and proceeded to clean it with his hankie. After putting it back in he turned to the Queen and asked 'Is it in straight?'

Aristotle Onassis (1906-75)

Had a massive lounge on his yacht. The footrests on the barstools were made of polished whales' teeth and the stools themselves covered with the skin of a whale's penis. (This led one wag to remark, 'Does this mean I'm sitting on Moby's dick?')

Bette Davis (1908-89)

Was in the habit of eating food with her hands instead of using knives and forks. 'I like to rip the guts out of fish,' she exclaimed on one occasion, 'I like to feel the goo and blood because it reminds me of all the people who've dumped on me.'

Mario Lanza (1921-59)

Once pulled off the underwear of actress Inger Stevens, spread her legs apart and crooned an aria into her vagina with the words, 'For the first time, Lanza's high notes will come out of a *woman's* body.'

David Lynch (1946-)

The director of *Blue Velvet* and other warped *noirish* classics has a bottle in his house containing a uterus which he received from a friend of his who had had a hysterectomy. She asked the surgeon to keep it as she felt he'd like it. It now accompanies Lynch's prized collection of fossilised animal parts and organic matter, which includes an excised pancreas, sclerosed kidneys and an amputated, gangrenous foot.

Tommy Bolt

This American pro golfer (winner of the U.S. Open in 1958) was notorious for breaking wind as he played. Indeed, he was fined $100 in the 1950s during one tournament for the habit. 'It wasn't just the farting that bothered us,' a tournament official told him afterwards, 'It was the fact that you kept lifting your leg and slapping your thigh in celebration as you did so.'

GRUMPS & GROUCHES

Diogenes (412-322BC)

Arguably history's first official eccentric, the founder of the Cynics is famous for sitting in a tub in Athens, occasionally bursting into ribald song ('It's all the people are interested in') and replying to anything people said to him by breaking wind in their direction.

He spent a day begging in front of a statue. When asked why he was doing this he replied, 'To prepare myself for the rejection I shall receive from human beings.' Diogenes also wandered about the streets in broad daylight armed with a lantern. Asked about his motive for this he said 'I'm looking for an honest man but haven't found one yet'.

Voltaire (1694-1778)

When visitors bored him the French author and philosopher simulated fainting fits to get rid of them.

Herbert Spencer (1820-1903)

If the evolutionary philosopher got bored with the conversation of his guests, he used to put in ear-plugs to signify the fact.

Johannes Brahms (1833-97)

A rude man by nature, he once said to a gathering after an evening in their company, 'If there is anyone here whom I have not insulted, I beg his pardon.'

Nick Goodall (1849-84)

Moody New York violinist who refused to play in concerts when he had something better to do (like shooting pool). He often took up to 20 minutes to tune his violin on stage, enjoying the frustration of the audiences as they waited.

Once he got going, however, there was no stopping him. On at least one occasion he continued playing long after the audience had departed, the night watchman had fallen asleep and fringes of the sun were visible on the horizon. He much preferred improvising in taverns where he could truly express himself without having to worry about impressing music snobs – or his bank manager – so it's hardly surprising he died in the poorhouse, a victim of his own temperamental genius.

Kirk Douglas (1916-)

If a party went on too long at his house he would simply go upstairs, change into his pyjamas, come down again and start flicking the lights on and off repeatedly to give his guests a not-so-gentle hint that it was time to go.

Dean Martin (1917-1995)

When he was bored at his own parties he used to ring the police anonymously to complain about the noise to get them finished.

Philip Larkin (1922-85)

Often a waspish individual, Larkin found it difficult to conceal his intellectual snobbery in his capacity as librarian at Hull University. If he saw someone taking out a lowbrow book he would often bark at them, 'Why on earth are you borrowing drivel like that?'

Robert Maxwell (1923-91)

The media magnate was once told to leave a flight from Mexico City to Acapulco because it was over-booked but refused to do so even when a Mexican policeman pointed a revolver at his stomach and told him he was going to shoot him if he didn't get off the plane. Always a persistent man, if people disagreed with him he badgered them with phone calls in the middle of the night until they came round to his way of thinking. Maxwell fired so many people he often forgot who was still working for him, so if you stayed on the premises after being told to go you might well have got away with it.

F.W. Denham

Cornish rector who died in 1953, having set many tongues wagging in his parish at Warleggan on account of his quixotic habits, which included dining chiefly on nettles and porridge. Denham took pains to avoid his parishioners, surrounding the rectory with barbed wire, cancelling appointments if they were one minute late, and picking fights with most of them on flimsy pretexts. When his congregation dwindled to one, he filled the vacant pews with cardboard cut-out models of the entire community.

HYPOCHONDRIACS

Lady Lewson (1700-96)

A leading light in London society, Lady Lewson became widowed at 26, thereafter developing some weird notions. She refused to clean windows, for instance, for fear that they would break, or that she would be somehow injured in the process. She also believed that moving furniture round a room could lead to health problems, as could washing oneself. She smeared her face and neck with pigs' fat to keep herself healthy. Judging by her longevity, maybe Lady Lewson knew something we don't.

Queen Victoria (1819-1901)

Victoria used to summon her physician to her side four or five times a day complaining of imaginary digestive problems.

Florence Nightingale (1820-1910)

After returning from the Crimean War in 1856, she developed the notion that she had terminal heart disease, and that her life hung by a thread – a belief she clung to with some passion for the next 54 years of good health.

Herbert Spencer (1820-1903)

The evolutionary philosoper often stopped a carriage in mid-journey (and often in mid-traffic too) to take his pulse. If he wasn't happy with it, he did a U-turn for home and summoned his doctor.

Louis Pasteur (1822-95)

The chemist and microbiologist was so fanatical about hygiene that he refused to shake hands with people when he met them for fear of picking up bugs.

Oskar von Redwitz (1823-91)

The German poet and dramatist attended a doctor every day of his life after he reached 40.

The Comtesse de Noailles (1824-1908)

Highly-strung Eastbourne lady who inflicted a tortuous regime on her adopted daughter Maria. First off she decided Maria's school uniform was unhealthy and removed it from her, dressing her in Grecian tunics and sandals instead. That way, she declared, the air could circulate more freely round her body. She also arranged for a special cow to occupy the school grounds so Maria could be sure of having pure milk. Further, she had the trees in her garden cut down, fearing some nasty germs could emanate from the bark. And she had the school pond drained for fear that unhygienic beings lived there.

Equally worried about her own health as that of her daughter, the Comtesse (the French title was spurious, by the way) wrapped socks stuffed with squirrel fur round her head at night to keep bugs away, and covered her chest with the skin of a Norwegian wild cat for the same reason.

Enrico Caruso (1873-1921)

The Italian operatic tenor was so nervous about falling into ill health he carried all sorts of medication with him when he travelled. After a walk in the park he always took a bath and changed his clothes afterwards. When he slept, he put a mattress with pillows on it on the floor beside him as a buffer should he fall out in his sleep.

Don Herold (1889-1966)

This U.S. cartoonist had every heart test under the sun in the 1950s after complaining of thumping sensations assailing him at nights. The cause turned out to be the thermostat on his electric blanket.

Howard Hughes (1905-76)

The film producer, businessman and aviator later on became a hypochondriac recluse. He paid his staff with cheques he floated down to them from an upstairs window for fear of contracting germs, and collected his post by means of a bucket lowered on a rope to the ground. He never allowed his doctor to touch him unless it was absolutely necessary. His barber also had a difficult job: Hughes made him use 36 combs, each of which had to be sterilised at every second stroke, and discarded after two minutes. He refused to touch door knobs for fear of infection, which meant he had to kick the bathroom door to let his aides know he wanted to enter it. If they didn't hear, he urinated on the floor. None of the aides were allowed to use his bathroom. If they were taken short, they were instructed to relieve themselves in empty milk cartons.

Joan Crawford (1906-77)

Whenever she entered a new home, the first thing she did was remove all the bathtubs, feeling it was unsanitary to sit in one's dirty bathwater.

George Hamilton (1939-)

Hamilton who camped up Dracula in the spoof movie, *Love at First Bite*, has a private blood bank in his house in case he injures himself and needs an immediate transfusion.

IDENTITY CRISES

Joshua Norton (1819-1880)

Born in London, this lovable nutcase went on to declare himself the self-appointed Emperor of the United States in a move to put an end to low standards in high places. He made himself Emperor of California in 1856 and three years later extended his 'reign' to the whole of the U.S. He printed his own money, attended every session of the Senate and when Maximillian assumed the throne of Mexico, sentenced him to death as an usurper.

Deciding that democracy was death to principles – 'the aristocracy of blackguards' in Lord Byron's phrase – he advocated a return to benign dictatorship, with himself at the helm. He thereby single-handedly abolished Congress, deposed the sitting President and announced that henceforth he and he alone would rule the vast continent. When Civil War broke out, he even summoned Abraham Lincoln to his dingy lodging-house to discuss what should be done to alleviate the situation. Lincloln declined the invitation.

In less turbulent times Norton paraded about the streets in a blue military uniform with golden epaulettes, salaaming the people who took him to their hearts and addressed him as 'Your Majesty'.

Robert Mitchum (1917-97)

Always referred to himself as an actress rather than an actor. Asked why, he replied, 'What's the difference? This is a profession where a dog, Rin Tin Tin, is a star.'

Norma Lambeck

This lady was robbed in Disneyland in 1978 and afterwards taken 'backstage' by the staff, who commiserated with her. When she was there she saw various Disney characters removing the heads from their costumes and was dismayed that they were not the animals they purported to represent. She took Disney plc to court for the distress she suffered in this sad realisation but the judge ruled that there was no onus on Disneyland to hide the truth of the real identity of Mickey Mouse & Co.

IGNORANCE

Dr Samuel Johnson (1709-84)

Despite his brilliance in literary matters, Dr Johnson was unable to tell the time by looking at a clock.

John Barrett

Eighteenth-century Vice-Provost of Trinity College, Dublin, who once made two holes at the bottom of his door for his pet cats, one large one and one somewhat smaller. For some reason it didn't strike him that the large hole would also have sufficed for the smaller cat!

Charles Darwin (1809-82)

Darwin's father told him he would end up disgracing his whole family because he performed so poorly at school. Darwin went on to study medicine in Edinburgh, then biology in Cambridge and is now remembered as the leader in the field of evolutionary biology after his epoch-making work *On the Origin of Species by Means of Natural Selection*.

Queen Victoria (1819-1901)

Was completely unaware of the phenomenon of lesbianism until an anti-homosexual bill was presented to her. Even then she went into denial about it, removing all references to the practice which meant in effect that while the bill criminalised homosexuality, it left lesbianism legal.

Menelik II (1844-1913)

This Ethiopian emperor imported an electric chair from America to execute local criminals but forgot that Ethiopia didn't have electricity when he made the purchase and ended up using it as a throne instead.

David Lloyd George (1863-1945)

During the 1919 Versailles Peace Conference, the then Prime Minister informed the Italian government that the best way it could boost its economy was by increasing its banana crop. One thing he overlooked was that Italy doesn't *grow* bananas.

Sam Goldwyn (1882-1974)

This legendary Hollywood producer was noted for foot-in-mouth disease. Presented with *The Diaries of Raoul de Sales, 1938-42* as a possible film option, he commented, 'The guy is four years old and he's keeping *diaries*?'

Nora Barnacle (1884-1951)

Though married to James Joyce, Nora hadn't a clue what any of his books were about and always felt he would have made a better singer than a writer.

Irving Berlin (1888-1989)

The Russian-born American composer who helped to launch 20th-century popular music, and was famed for musicals such as *Annie Get Your Gun*, always claimed he could never read music.

Robert Benchley (1889-1945)

The American writer seemed to be unaware of Venice's canal system and after his arrival there to do a drama piece for *The New Yorker* he sent a telegram to his editor that went: 'Streets Full of Water. Please advise.'

Dorothy Parker (1893-1967)

Once bought a new typewriter because the ribbon on her old model ran out and she didn't know how to fit a new one on.

INNOVATIONS

Leonardo da Vinci (1452-1519)

A man of many talents, da Vinci is primarily remembered today as a painter but he was also a musician, architect, military engineer, scientist and, last but not least, an inventor. He once designed a tank with sloping sides to shield it against artillery, and worked on plans for several flying machines. The most notable of these he called a 'ship of the air': it had four flapping wings which the pilot operated by pushing against a pole. He also designed a parachute. His military inventions included a rapid-firing cannon and a giant crossbow, and he even drew up detailed instructions for making stink bombs. These and other plans were made in 'mirror writing' (i.e. from right to left on the page) over thousands of pages, most of them unpublished until after his death. He even invented an alarm clock which woke people up by rubbing their feet.

Richard Pockrich (c.1695-1759)

The unpredictable inventor born in Co. Monaghan, Ireland was left £4000 by his father, which gave him the wherewithal to indulge some of his scattier schemes. He tried to turn Eccles Mount into a cake house but the owner refused, despite Richard's attempt to bribe him with presents of pigeons. His scheme to turn bogland into vineyards was abandoned as fruitless, as was his subsequent dream of providing every Irishman with a pair of stick-on wings so the whole nation could fly to work every day.

His most successful invention was a musical instrument which consisted of tumblers full of water; you played a melody by running wet fingers round the rims of the glasses. This idea impressed Benjamin Franklin so much that he developed his own 120-glass Armonica on which he played music composed for the occasion by Mozart and Beethoven.

Tobias Smollett (1721-71)

The Scottish author invented the post box.

Jemmy Hirst (1738-1829)

This farmer from Rawcliffe dabbled with inventing and came up with a windmill that could slice turnips as it turned. He also created a wickerwork carriage which was first pulled by his bull Jupiter, and was then drawn by Andalusian mules. Later he attached sails to it so that the wind could drive it. He drove off in this strange contraption dressed in multi-coloured hunting gear and a broad-brimmed hat to visit King George III who was intrigued by stories he had heard of the inventor. Hirst gave the King a tour of his carriage and showed him the clock he had invented to measure distance travelled. He made a point of showing the King the barrel he had installed for containing wine. This was empty. The King refilled it and sent him on his way. Hirst told him it had been a pleasure to meet such a plain old man and he was welcome at Rawcliffe any time.

Thomas Jefferson (1743-1826)

The third president of the United States who drafted the Declaration of Independence is less well-known as the inventor of the coathanger.

Sir Francis Galton (1822-1911)

The 19th-century scientist invented a very practical device: a warning signal in his dining-room to let the guests know when somebody was in the toilet. 'It saves a futile climb upstairs.' he explained, 'and the occupant isn't subjected to the embarrassment of having the door handle rattled.'

Princess Marie (1825-89)

Daughter-in-law of Queen Victoria who developed the notion that left and right-footed shoes were not a good idea. Instead she opted for the much more practical variety which suited either foot – a marketing ploy yet to be exploited.

Alexander Graham Bell (1847-1922)

Though deaf, Bell still managed to invent the telephone.

Thomas Edison (1847-1931)

As well as the phonograph, Edison invented a sewing machine that could be powered by the human voice. The idea was that you roared at it non-stop and it did its business ... but he didn't perfect the device and some of the roars that ensued had a different cause. Finally, after seeing his colleagues succumb to a succession of sore throats, he dropped the idea.

Sir George Reresby Sitwell (1860-1943)

Head of the eccentric Sitwell family, antiquarian and genealogist, Sir George also had a slew of decidedly odd inventions to his credit, like for instance the musical toothbrush, and a revolver that killed wasps.

Salvador Dali (1904-89)

Dali devised shoes with springs in them to enhance the pleasure of walking, and artificial fingers made of mirrors. He once tried to interest Paris shop-owners in transparent mannikins whose bodies were filled with water and goldfish.

Walter Langstaff

British inventor who patented a golf ball in 1912 that was made from the dried-out skin of a bull's penis.

Margaret Thatcher (1925-)

As a young woman Thatcher developed a method of mixing more air into ice-cream so that customers paid more for less.

Merlin Maddock

This former locomotive engineer from South Wales devoted the seminal years of his life to inventing slightly crazy items like harps made from carbon fire, ponds from jet engines, chairs with spring-loaded seats, house lights operated by foot switches and even a wooden penny farthing bicycle which he once rode blindfolded over the Severn Bridge. He also tried to ride it to London in the 1980s to see Margaret Thatcher, but was knocked off it by a photographer in Bristol and had to get the train to Paddington, cycling from there to Downing Street to see the Iron Lady.

The aptly-named Merlin also invented a mobile phone with an ordinary circular dial and handset which comes in a large suitcase and is operated by means of an aerial, and a waistcoat that generates heat everytime the wearer chuckles or sneezes. At Christmas, he used to hang his tree upside down from the ceiling, placing an open umbrella underneath it so that the pine needles wouldn't be all over the carpet. An added benefit of this (one of his more practical ideas) was that presents could be stored so close to the ceiling that children wouldn't be able to open them prematurely.

Jake Mangol Wurzle

This American invented a new style of motorbike which had a fan on the front to keep pedestrians at a safe distance. It also had a metal pole that acted as a lightning conductor, a basket on the back for his dog and an added device upon which he hung his washing. His invention didn't impress the police however, and he appeared at St. Alban's court in the 1980s on a charge of driving a dangerous vehicle.

INSPIRATION

Robert Schumann (1810-56)

The German composer claimed he often got ideas for his scores from his imaginary friends: Florestan and Eusebius.

Lewis Carroll (1832-98)

Wrote his first poem at the age of 13. Asked how he managed to compose it, he replied blithely, 'I had a fairy by my side'.

Maurice Ravel (1875-1937)

The French composer of Basque origins, who rebelliously experimented with the rules of harmony and syncopation, was inspired to write *Bolero* after a trip to a noisy steel mill.

Mack Sennett (1880-1960)

This Canadian-born creator of *The Keystone Cops* said he got his best inspiration for movies in the bathtub so eventually had one installed in the middle of his office.

Pablo Picasso (1881-1973)

Had Gertrude Stein pose over 80 times for his famous portrait of her in 1906 but found himself getting nowhere with it as the inspiration was lacking. He finally trashed it, and went off to Spain, where he finished it from his mind's eye. 'It was only when I stopped looking at you that I really saw you,' he informed her.

Raymond Chandler (1888-1959)

Asked his wife to do the housework in the nude because it gave him inspiration for his writing.

Salvador Dali (1904-89)

Used to gorge himself on cheese before he went to bed as he felt it made him dream in ways he could later visualise in his work. Got so much of his inspiration from dreams that each night when he went to bed he left unfinished paintings at the bottom of it, hoping that when he woke up the next morning the

manner of its completion would immediately suggest
itself to him.

Jackie Collins (1941-)

To get material for her books she specialised in going
to glitzy parties and earwigging the conversations,
then going into the loo and jotting down what she
heard in notebooks before she forgot. 'I love her,' says
Angie Dickinson, 'but that doesn't mean I trust her. I
mean, she'll take notes right in front of me.'

KILLERS

Prince Vlad III (Dracula)

The 15th-century tyrant known as Vlad the Impaler,
who was the inspiration for Bram Stoker's Dracula,
liked to drink the blood of his victims. He also often
forced women to eat the cooked flesh of their
husbands after he'd murdered them. When some
Turkish emissaries to his palace forgot to remove their
fezzes upon entering, he nailed them to their heads as
a punishment.

Mahomet III (1566-1603)

Despotic sultan of the Ottoman Empire who had all
19 of his brothers executed on the night he acceded to

the throne, just to ensure there wouldn't be any sibling rivalry. Problems from possible step-brothers or sisters were obviated when he went into his late father's harem and, locating seven pregnant ladies, had them tied up in weighted sacks and dropped into the Bosphorus.

Adahoozou I

This 16th-century king of Dahomey in West Africa had the walls of his city lined with the decapitated heads of his enemies. Informed by the builders that there was still some wall space available, he ordered them to find more heads quickly or he would use theirs. The task, not surprisingly, was completed in record time.

Murad IV (1612-40)

The sultan of the Ottoman Empire was so ruthless he had his chief musician beheaded for playing a Persian tune. He once had a group of picnickers drowned because they were making too much noise. He banned tobacco entirely and when he caught one of his gardeners and his wife lighting up, he showed exactly how bad for you smoking can be: he had their legs cut off and then wheeled the pair of them through the streets until they bled to death.

Queen Zingua

Seventeenth-century queen of Angola who was reputed to have tortured and subsequently crippled the men in her life 'because cripples make the best lovers'. She also arranged duels to the death between warriors, going to bed with the winner and then having him killed the following morning. She continued copulating and killing until the age of 77 when she converted to Catholicism.

Nasur-Ud-Din (1831-96)

The former Shah of Persia, during a visit to an English prison, asked if he could see someone being hanged. After being informed that an execution wasn't scheduled for that day, he offered one of his own men so that the spectacle could be arranged.

Mata Hari (1876-1917)

When she learned she was about to be executed, the famous Dutch dancer, who spied for the Germans during World War Two, killed her favourite pony by thrusting a stiletto into its heart because she didn't want anyone else to have it after she was gone.

John George Haigh

Known as the 'Acid Bath Vampire', Yorkshire-born Haigh murdered nine people in the Surrey area in 1949 by opening their veins with a penknife, tapping off glassfuls of blood and then drinking it. He then disposed of their bodies in acid baths, believing that if there was no corpse, there could be no conviction. Unfortunately he was wrong and the police assembled a considerable body of evidence against him and he *was* convicted. He also liked drinking urine, citing the biblical 'He that believeth in me, the Scripture hath said, out of his belly shall flow rivers of living water'.

Luigi Longhi

This Danish serial killer was convicted in 1983 and sent to a mental home after a trial which heard evidence that Longhi not only murdered women but also washed their hair repeatedly before he did so, using honey, cottage cheese and vegetable dressing if he ran out of shampoo.

Denis Nielson

This serial killer is now in prison, having been convicted in 1983 of some of the most horrific murders ever committed in Britain. A homosexual, he often killed men he had relationships with when he felt those relationships were about to end. After killing his victims he used to keep them under the floorboards of his house, and take them out and dance with them when he felt like it.

LAWS

Claudius (10BC-AD54)

The Roman emperor passed a law sanctioning the breaking of wind at the table after hearing of a man who became ill from resisting the urge due to politeness.

King Canute (994-1035)

The King of England decreed that the ears and noses of adulterous women should be cut off.

Pope Eugenius III

Had the misfortune to visit Paris on a Friday in 1147. Since this was a fasting day for Catholics, the atmosphere was rather muted, but the pontiff had a brainwave. A Papal decree was issued to say that this particular Friday was a Thursday and festivities ensued.

Edward III (1312-77)

The English king passed a law making it illegal for anyone to eat more than two meals a day.

Joanna I

Fourteenth-century Queen of Naples who issued a decree that no man must force his wife to have sex more than six times a day.

Catherine de Medici (1519-89)

Queen of France who decreed that all women at the French court had to have waists less than 22 centimetres in width.

Queen Elizabeth I (1533-1603)

Once passed a law prohibiting everyone except the rich to wear flat caps on Sundays, and another taxing men with beards. Yet another act passed under the reign of Elizabeth declared that 'Any woman who through the use of false hair, Spanish hair pads, make-up, false hips, steel busks, panniers, high-heeled shoes or other devices, leads a subject of Her Majesty into marriage, shall be punished with the penalties of witchcraft.'

Pope Urban III

Threatened to execute snuff users in 1624, deeming it a disgusting habit.

Oliver Cromwell (1599-1658)

This killjoy made Ebeneezer Scrooge look like St. Nicholas when he 'abolished' Christmas in 1649, making it an ordinary working day instead. Those who insisted on contravening his orders were thrown into prison for their temerity.

James II (1622-1701)

To boost the wool trade he issued an edict that everyone be buried in a woollen shroud. The law was only repealed in 1814.

Louis XIV (1638-1715)

The French king prohibited everyone in his palace from sitting in chairs with arms in them, reserving that right for himself and his queen.

Peter the Great (1672-1725)

This enterprising Russian Tsar once placed a tax on beards to raise money for the Treasury when he had exhausted other ideas. Men who stayed in their villages were free of the burden, but if they travelled to other towns or cities they were liable to pay for their facial hair. Upon payment, discs were attached to the beards so they wouldn't have to fork out twice.

Paul I (1754-1801)

Another Russian Tsar decreed that anyone who mentioned his baldness (which perturbed him greatly) would be flogged to death.

Amanullah Khan (1822-1960)

Afghanistan king who tried to pass a law requiring all his male subjects to wear bowler hats. His zeal for westernising provoked unrest and he fled to foreign shores in 1929.

Shaka

Nineteenth-century Zulu king whose rule was so strict that he made sneezing, coughing and breaking wind crimes punishable by death.

Fred Williams

Republican politician who, in 1984 in Missouri, introduced a bill to prohibit nose-blowing in restaurants if done in a 'loud, obnoxious or offensive manner'. Infringers were subject to a $200 fine.

LITERARY LOONS

Thomas Hobbes (1588-1679)

Wrote most of his natural philosophy tracts lying in bed. If he ran out of paper he resorted to the sheets – or even his legs.

Jonathan Swift (1667-1745)

The author of *Gulliver's Travels* was known as 'the mad parson' in the parish where he was rector due to his appearance and his odd behaviour. He was notoriously irritable and misogynistic, claiming that women were of a species 'hardly a degree above a monkey'. He was obsessed with exercise, imagining it would protect him from disease, and sometimes walked up to ten miles a day. If it was raining, he ran up and down the stairs repeatedly to exercise his muscles. In his later days he ate his meals whilst walking around his room. As his mind deteriorated, his manservants were cruel enough to charge people a fee to come and see the 78-year-old senile writer pacing around for amusement.

Jeremy Bentham (1748-1832)

The English philosopher and social reformer who invented the 'Panopticon', a type of prison where the prisoner is under constant surveillance, also had hundreds of scatterbrained schemes and misconceived inventions, many of which he tried to jot down on tiny bits of paper, but his hand rarely kept up with his mind and most were indecipherable.

William Blake (1757-1827)

Known as 'the Cockney nutcase' in his lifetime and appreciated only after his death, Blake only goes to show how fine the line between madness and genius is. Many of his paintings were inspired by visions such as angels in a tree on Peckham Rye. He had an ambition of walking to the horizon and trying to touch the sky with his finger and held imaginary conversations with Julius Caesar.

William Wordsworth (1770-1850)

Never wrote a line of poetry during the seven years that he was Poet Laureate. He once wallpapered a whole room with newspapers. The poet took so many notes while roaming the hills and dales of the Lake District that he was suspected of being a French spy and was shadowed for a month by a detective.

Charles Robert Maturin

Irish clergyman of Huguenot descent who was born in 1782. He was also a playwright and novelist of some note. His reputation rested mainly on his magnum opus *Melmoth the Wanderer*, a novel he submitted to publishers in a heap of unnumbered pages which were mostly out of order. When he wasn't at his writing desk he had some unusual habits such as wearing evening dress while fishing or keeping the shutters on his room closed all day so that he wouldn't be able to differentiate between day and night. He painted the ceiling of his house with cloud designs to give the impression he was sleeping outside, and decorated the walls with murals featuring scenes from his novels.

He often called on people in his dressing-gown and slippers, or wearing a shoe on one foot and a boot on the other. When he felt the urge to write he put a wafer

on his forehead: his family knew this was a signal to steer clear of him.

Honoré de Balzac (1799-1850)

Used coffee to awaken his muse, consuming vast quantities from midnight until dawn, which was when he did most of his writing. 'It falls into your stomach,' he said, 'and straight away there is a general commotion. Ideas begin to move like the battalions of the Grand Army on the battlefield. The struggle commences and is concluded with torrents of black water.'

Alfred, Lord Tennyson (1809-92)

The melancholic Victorian poet was not always so serious: his party piece was an impersonation of a man sitting and straining on a lavatory.

J.M. Barrie (1860-1937)

When his elder brother died in a skating accident his mother was distraught. To bring her out of her depression he dressed up as the other boy and even imitated his voice.

Maurice Baring (1874-1945)

This wayward English novelist and one-time c orrespondent for *The Times* would sit at the dinner table with a glass of port perched on top of his head. A woman handed him a glass with whiskey in it one night at a party, asking him to balance it likewise and he replied. 'I'm sorry - I can only do it with port'.

To celebrate his birthday every year he jumped fully clothed into a river. He bought a coat one day to go on a train journey but when he discovered it didn't fit into his briefcase he threw it out the window of the train in disgust.

G.K. Chesterton (1874-1934)

To cure writer's block he used to take an arrow from a quiver, get out his bow and fire it through a window at a tree in his garden.

Gertrude Stein (1874-1946)

This doyenne of experimental writing refused to use punctuation in her work. She especially disliked commas, remarking, 'A comma by helping you along holding your coat for you and putting on your shoes keeps you from living your life as actively as you should lead it.'

Franz Kafka (1883-1924)

Deliberately left letters addressed to him unopened for long periods of time as he feared receiving any bad news.

T.S. Eliot (1888-1965)

The American-born poet once took to painting his face green. He also insisted at one stage that he be addressed as 'Captain' though he had no nautical experience.

J.D. Salinger (1919-)

Ever the purist, he refused an editor's request to change the title of *The Catcher in the Rye* because he felt Holden Caulfield (its main character) wouldn't have approved.

When his daughter Margaret was sick, he refused to allow her traditional medical attention. A convert to Christian Science, he insisted instead on his own prescriptions for homeopathic cures, and acupuncture with wooden rods. He also drank his own urine, and started speaking in tongues in a church after a charismatic renewal service.

Truman Capote (1924-84)

Hated writing so much he postponed it by sharpening and resharpening pencils for hours at a time, sometimes reaching a tally of up to 500. When he finally did start he used yellow paper for his first draft, white for his second and then typed the third and final one. He never veered from this *modus operandi*.

George Perec

The French author wrote a book called *La Disparition* (Avoid) which didn't use the letter 'e'. This was equalled by his English translater Gilbert Adair who managed to replicate the feat. (Perec also wrote a novel which contains no other vowels except 'e'.)

Jerzy Andrezejewski

The Polish novelist published a book in 1962 called *The Gates of Paradise* which was written as one single sentence with its 40,000 words containing no punctuation at all.

THE MACABRE

Pedro I (1320-69)

This Portuguese prince was unlucky in love: his first two wives died prematurely and his third, Inez de Castro, was murdered in 1355 by arrangement of his father Alfonso, who had discovered she was illegitimate and, so he thought, not worthy of his son. Two years later when Pedro acceded to the throne, he tracked down the three assassins, imprisoned them and then had their hearts ripped out. He also exhumed the corpse of his murdered wife, dressed her in her royal apparel, seated her on a throne and had her crowned as his queen. Members of his court were obliged to kiss her hand. After the ceremony, he had the corpse and throne sealed in a marble sarcophagus.

Queen Juana of Spain

Juana was so heartbroken when her husband died in 1506 that she refused to have him buried and brought his coffin everywhere she went.

Walter Raleigh (1552-1618)

For 20 years after his execution his wife kept the writer's head in a red velvet bag.

Samuel Pepys (1663-1703)

Not only was he fond of chasing young ladies, Pepys couldn't keep his hands off dead ones either: he kissed and fondled the mummified corpse of Catherine de Valois in Westminster Abbey on his 36th birthday.

Lord Byron (1788-1824)

When Byron was in his late teens and staying at a monastery with friends, the whole group would dress up as monks and drink burgundy from a monk's skull which they had dug up in the grounds.

John Alington (1795-1863)

Hertfordshire rector known as 'Mad Jack' who liked to be carried round his garden in an open coffin to prepare himself for his eventual demise.

Lady Adeline Cardigan

The 18th-century hunting lady, the wife of the 7th Earl of Cardigan, after whom the clothing item was named, had her death mask made at the time her husband died: she was relatively young (and would live for a further 40 years or so), but was vain and wanted to be remembered forever as youthful. She also had a coffin made many years before she died and would bring it out to show visitors.

Sarah Bernhardt (1844-1923)

The great French actress was so obsessed with death that she made it a practice to visit morgues to view the unclaimed corpses of derelicts that had been dragged from the river Seine. As a teenager she also persuaded her mother to buy her a rosewood coffin lined with white satin. She often slept in this as a young woman, both alone and with her lovers. She also used the coffin as a table upon which she served tea and even took it on tours with her.

Truman Capote (1924-84)

At one point in his life the author frequented a necrophiliac bar in Greenwich Village in New York where people who wanted to have sex with the dead exchanged addresses of funeral parlours.

Elvis Presley (1935-77)

Elvis was fascinated with corpses and used to visit the Memphis morgue to gaze at the bodies. He felt he would die young and at times looked forward to death, as it meant he would be reunited with his mother, whom he loved more than any woman he ever met.

MARRIAGE

Cleopatra (69-30BC)

The offspring of a liaison between a brother and a sister, she actually married two of her own brothers as well.

Elagabalus

Mad Roman emperor of the third century AD who 'married' Hierocles, one of his gay lovers, after shaving his chin and having the remaining hairs plucked out to make himself look more like a woman. The honeymoon consisted of Hierocles beating him senseless, Elagabalus being a raving masochist as well. Anybody who expressed concern over such a state of affairs – or rather such affairs of state – was executed. Eventually, however, his soldiers rose up against him and slew both him and Hierocles. Their bodies were dragged through the city, mutilated and thrown into the sewers which ran into the river Tiber.

Ethelred (968-1016)

This English king took not only his bride with him on his honeymoon but her mother as well ... and slept with the mother.

Philip II (1165-1223)

On his wedding day in 1193, this French king decided that he wasn't really in love with his new bride after all so he put her in a nunnery just after the reception ended and ordered her to remain there.

Giovanni Casanova (1725-98)

The Italian adventurer and philanderer was about to marry a woman called Leonilda when he suddenly realised she was his own daughter from an age-old affair.

Martin van Butchell (1735-1812)

This Englishman's wife had a clause inserted in their marriage contract stating that as soon as she was buried, her estate should pass to one of her relatives. Instead of burying her, Martin had her embalmed and placed in a glass-topped case which he kept in his drawing-room. He called her 'The Preserved Lady' and proudly exhibited her to visitors. When he re-married, however, his new wife insisted that she be removed from the house so he had her delivered to the Royal College of Surgeons in London. She remained there until that building was bombed during the Second World War.

Marie Antoinette (1755-93)

Didn't consummate her marriage with Louis XVI until seven years after the wedding.

Brigham Young (1801-77)

This esteemed 19th-century Mormon led the trek to Utah where he founded Salt Lake City and became the governor. He had between 30 and 70 wives, according to different reports of his life. He was polygamous because he believed (conveniently for himself) that such a state eliminated prostitution, spinsterhood and adultery, and also, of course, increased the Mormon fold. Having said that, he wasn't exactly monkish with his spouses. When a few of them were under the same roof as he was for the night, he was in the habit of putting chalkmarks outside the door of his chosen one for that evening. He drank vast quantities of milk, believing this to be an aid to fertility: he had approximately 56 children.

Leopold II (1835-1909)

Belgian king who married his mistress prior to a serious operation, introducing her to the best man after the ceremony as his widow. (He was prescient, as she attained that status a few days later.)

Sigmund Freud (1865-1939)

The founder of psychoanalysis was so cossetted by his wife, she even put the toothpaste on his brush for him.

Stan Laurel (1890-1965)

Married eight times, but three of his wives (his second, third and seventh) were the same person: Virginia Rogers.

Aristotle Onassis (1906-75)

His marriage certificate to Jacqueline Kennedy had 173 clauses. One of them was that the couple would have no children; another that they would sleep in separate bedrooms. Jackie was to get £6000 a month for clothes and, if Onassis decided to leave her, £6 million for every year of their marriage.

William Saroyan (1908-81)

The American playwright and novelist married Carol Marcus in 1943, divorced her in 1949, married her again in 1951 and re-divorced her the following year.

Jean Acker

The lesbian first wife of Rudolph Valentino locked him out of the boudoir on their wedding night in 1919. The marriage lasted less than six hours. She was annoyed, apparently, because he refused to carry her over the threshold.

MARRIAGE PROPOSALS

Ninon de Lenclos (1620-1705)

French courtesan who was proposed to by her own son, he being unaware she was his mother. When she told him the truth he was so devastated he stabbed himself to death with his sword.

Benjamin Disraeli (1804-1881)

When he was 69 he became infatuated with a married woman called Lady Bradford, who rebuffed his advances. He proposed marriage to her 71-year-old sister to be near her but this offer was also rejected.

Thomas Edison (1847-1931)

The inventor and physicist proposed to his wife on a train journey using morse code.

W.B. Yeats (1865-1939)

Proposed marriage to Maud Gonne MacBride umpteen times, with each overture being rejected out of hand. Finally, out of desperation, he also proposed to her (illegitimate) daughter Iseult. This too was rejected.

Fiorello La Guardia

Former New York Mayor who married his secretary Marie Fischer in 1929 because she was so good at her job. His marriage proposal went as follows: 'Files are the curse of modern civilisation. If you can keep my ones up to date, I'll marry you'. Overcome by his romantic overture, she accepted.

Charles Bukowski (1920-94)

The American writer proposed marriage to Texan Court clerk Barbara Frye half in jest in a letter he wrote to her in 1955. She had accepted some poems of his for a magazine she edited and they built up an epistolary relationship. In one letter she said she thought she would never get a man to marry her because she had been born with two vertebrae missing, which meant she had to turn her whole body round when she wanted to look sideways. 'I'll marry you!' Bukowski wrote in reply, and she took him up on his offer, ditching her job and travelling up from Texas to where he lived and ditching her job. They were married the day after they met but divorced after two years.

Bob Caston

This journalist proposed to his girlfriend in his column in the *Saratoga Sun* in 1982. Not to be outdone, she replied in the affirmative to his request in a letter to the editor.

MARVELLOUS MEDICINE

Demosthenes (?-412BC)

This Athenian general tried to cure a speech impediment by putting pebbles in his mouth.

Pliny the Elder (AD23-79)

Had unusual ideas about contraception and believed that if you took two small worms out of the body of a certain species of spider and attached them in a piece of deer's skin to a woman's body before dawn, she wouldn't conceive. Aetios of Amida (527-565) went one better by suggesting that a man should wash his penis in vinegar or brine, while a woman should wear a cat's testicle in a tube across her navel to prevent conception. The Greek physician Soranus (98-138) had an even more detailed solution to the problem, recommending that when a man climaxed, the woman should 'hold her breath, draw her body back a little so the semen cannot penetrate, then immediately get up and sit down with bent knees and sneeze'.

Nero (AD37-68)

Nero developed a taste for music early on and often performed for the people of Rome – which was deemed highly inappropriate for an Emperor. Nero tried a variety of methods of improving his voice including lying on his back with a slab of lead on his chest, using enemas and emetics to keep his weight down, and refraining from apples and other food considered dangerous to the vocal chords.

Queen Elizabeth I (1533-1603)

When the queen contracted smallpox in 1562 she smeared her face with her own urine to cure it. She recovered from the illness, remaining unscarred.

Richard Pockrich (1695-1759)

This Irishman believed that life could be prolonged indefinitely by repeated blood transfusions. He felt that if the 'redundant' blood of old people was mixed with the vibrant blood of the young, life expectancy could be unlimited. He agreed however that if an individual attained the age of 999, it was only fair that an Act of Parliament decree that the person's assets accede to his or her descendants. More prosaically, Richard recommended people try to keep wrinkles away by steeping brown paper in vinegar and applying it to the face every half-hour.

John Wesley (1703-91)

Wesley, who founded Methodism, looked into cures for the body as well as the soul, and believed that the wearing of celandine leaves on the feet cured jaundice, and that if you swallowed three pounds of mercury, you could cure yourself of hernias.

Matthew Robinson (1712-1799)

Eighteenth-century MP, later titled Lord Rokeby, was also given the sobriquet 'the amphibious lord' because he believed so much in the curative powers of water that he spent hours immersed in it up to his neck. He used to go down to the sea each day and bathe, accompanied by a servant. Sometimes he stayed in so long he would pass out from the cold and the servant would have to rescue him. When the locals heard about this and went along to watch for fun, he afterwards took his dips in private in a large bath in a glasshouse, often eating his meals in this position and even writing political pamphlets from it. He was suspicious of doctors and was a firm believer in the healing powers of fresh air. He lived to 87.

Sir Robert Walpole (1717-97)

The former British Prime Minister swallowed over 180 pounds of soap once to try to get rid of a stone in his bladder.

Philip Thicknesse (1719-92)

The Northampton captain and travel writer suffered agonising pain from gallstones. He imagined he would cure them by riding his horse vigorously or driving his carriage over rough roads. He felt the pain was caused by the stones' rough edges and believed violent movement would knock off such edges and take the pain away.

Sylvester Graham (1794-1851)

A Presbyterian minister who waged war on drink, fatty food and meat, because he thought consumption of these would lead to unseemly sexual desire. Mustard and ketchup were even worse, he opined, and led to insanity. Every ejaculation a man had shortened his life, he preached, so it was of the utmost importance to practise chastity. (He recommended daily bowel movements as a practical antidote to boudoir-frolicking.) Sex, he contended, not only led to lassitude, depression and loss of appetite, but also headaches, melancholy, blindness, coughing, pulmonary consumption, spinal diseases, weakness of the brain, amnesia and epilepsy. If one engaged overmuch in carnal pursuits, the good minister continued, one's offspring would also die young.

Jonas Hanway

This 18th-century merchant from Tipping, author of 74 books and believed-to-be inventor of the umbrella, was averse to a good cuppa, believing that tea-drinking led to adultery, divorce and suicide.

William Ewart Gladstone (1809-98)

The four-times Prime Minister of Great Britain believed the best way to achieve longevity was to chew each morsel of food precisely 32 times.

Sir Francis Galton (1822-1911)

The 19th-century scientist and explorer, known for his studies of heredity and intelligence, who also came up with some home remedies. He believed that lice could be avoided by making little beads out of mercury and tea leaves and tying them in a loop round one's neck, and that treacle and lime juice spread on the gums would stop one's teeth falling out in cases of scurvy.

Sir Tatton Sykes (1826-1913)

This British aristocrat believed the body should be kept at the same temperature at all times in order that one remain in the peak of health. To this end, he wore six or seven coats when he set out walking, and discarded them one by one as he got hotter, dropping them on the side of the road. Local children would follow him and return the coats for a shilling apiece. Once when overcome by heat in a railway carriage he took off his shoes and socks and thrust his feet out of the window to the bewilderment of his fellow passengers.

Edward VII (1841-1910)

Strapped two sherry corks around his legs in the hope that it would cure his rheumatism.

Enrico Caruso (1873-1921)

The Italian tenor believed pulmonary complaints could be cured by wearing a dried anchovy as a necklace.

Marie Stopes (1880-1958)

This suffragette and pioneer advocate of birth control made her son walk around in a knitted skirt because she felt the rubbing of trousers against the genitals damaged them.

Vita Sackville-West (1892-1962)

Vita devised a method of curing sore throats which entailed tying a pair of old socks round one's neck.

R.D. Laing (1927-89)

The controversial Scottish psychiatrist had original methods of dealing with his patients. When one of them refused to put on her clothes to see him he decided to play her at her own game, and took off all his own clothes, interviewing her in the nude.

Princess Margaret (1930-)

After she scalded her feet in a bathroom accident, doctors used the ancient cure of placing maggots on her to eat her flesh when antibiotics failed to effect a remedy.

MASOCHISTS

Voltaire (1694-1778)

The French philosopher got such a thrill from receiving enemas that he carried the contraption with which they were administered everywhere with him.

Jean Jacques Rousseau (1712-78)

The 18th-century philosopher was a 'flasher', specialising in hiding in dark alleyways and mooning for ladies who passed by. He also took great pleasure in being flogged, as his infant teacher learned to her dismay. Rousseau also kissed items of furniture like tables and chairs when he was feeling elated.

Philip Thicknesse (1719-92)

The dilettante writer, and friend of artistic and society personalities such as Gainsborough, Thicknesse earned money at school by allowing other boys to beat him for so much per stroke.

William Ewart Gladstone (1809-98)

This politician visited brothels frequently, ostensibly to 'reform' the women but in actual fact to commune physically with them. Consumed with guilt afterwards, he whipped himself to exorcise it.

Fyodor Dostoevsky (1821-81)

The Russian novelist got a sexual thrill from being beaten and was even turned on by the miming of violence against him.

Leopold Von Sacher-Masoch (1836-95)

This Austrian author gave the world the word masochism. He first experienced pleasure at being beaten after his aunt caught him spying on her having sex and soundly thrashed him. In later years he paid women to beat him, giving them extra if they wore fur-lined clothes when doing so. His wife Wanda thrashed him every day of their 15-year marriage with a nail-studded whip. After she left him he married another woman, whom he tried to strangle. He eventually went insane.

James Joyce (1882-1941)

Had something of a persecution complex that almost gave him a need for betrayal. He wanted his wife Nora to have had affairs with other men before she met him and also during their time together so that he could revel in his image as a cuckold.

T.E. Lawrence (1888-1935)

Saw no essential difference between pleasure and pain, which meant that he was quite gratified by a beating he received from a Turk during the First World War. As he wrote in *Seven Pillars of Wisdom*, 'I remember smiling idly at him afterwards, for a delicious warmth, probably sexual, was swelling through me'. It was more than probable, and such beatings became a feature of his life for the next 12 years. When military enemies weren't available, he was happy to pay civilians to beat his bottom with metal whips, preferably while wearing spiked boots.

Oofty Goofty

Nobody knows the real name of this 19th-century American performer. He was recruited to a circus at a young age, being touted as a wild man recently captured from the jungles of Borneo and placed in a cage where he was fed huge chunks of meat and expected to prance about the place like King Kong, beating his chest and screaming cacophonously. He got his name as a result of his habit of shouting 'oofty-goofty' whenever anyone approached his cage. His next incarnation was as a singer at a Barbary Coast variety house. He was less successful at this and after his stint he usually got beaten up by the punters. He realised that he had an unusually high threshold for pain, and he decided to turn it to his advantage by offering to have himself beaten for money. He charged a dime to be kicked, a quarter to be hit with a walking stick and fifty cents to be whacked with a baseball bat. One day, however, in the late 1890s he allowed himself to be whacked with a billiard cue by the then-heavyweight boxing champion John L. Sullivan and the blow did irreparable damage to his back and ended his career. He died in obscurity, walking with a limp to the end of his days.

James Dean (1931-55)

The American actor was reputed to have had strong masochistic tendencies. He liked being burned with cigarettes – leading to his sobriquet 'The Human Ashtray' in underground circles.

Percy Grainger (1882-1961)

The Australian pianist was so addicted to flagellation he even brought whips on concert tours with him. He laundered his own shirts because of the profusion of blood stains on them that resulted from his masochistic exertions. 'A man cannot be a full artist unless he is manly,' he wrote to a friend in 1936, 'and a man can't be manly unless his sex life is selfish, brutal, wilful and unbridled'. Another hobby Percy had was lying naked and spreadeagled on top of his piano in the depths of winter with the windows open.

Roland Agret

When this Frenchman was arrested for murder in 1973, he vehemently protested his innocence. He was found guilty at his trial and after his conviction he swallowed forks, spoons and pens as part of his protest, and had to have three operations to have them removed. In 1974 he tried to hang himself and the following year went on a hunger strike. He was pardoned by President Giscard d'Estaing but wasn't happy with this, insisting that the conviction be overturned. In 1983, to expedite this, he cut off one of his little fingers and carried it to the Justice Ministry in a jar. A year later he did the same with his other little finger, and threatened to sew up his mouth and begin another hunger strike if he didn't get his wish. At this point the French legislature started to think the man meant business and acceded to his wishes.

MILITARY

Xerxes (c.519-465BC)

The Persian emperor attempted to invade Athens, but a storm blew up on the Hellespont and destroyed his fleet. Incensed, he ordered the sea to be whipped as a punishment.

Alexander the Great (356-323BC)

Alexander, the King of Macedonia, had helmets made for some of his soldiers which were far too large for their heads. He placed them strategically on battlefields to scare the wits out of the enemy, who thought they were facing enormous men. He also ordered all his troops to shave their beards off before battles so the enemy couldn't tug them.

George Osbaldeston (1786-1866)

In 1809 this tireless huntsman and soldier was made Lieutenant Colonel of the 5th Regiment of the North Riding Local Militia, astounding all his military colleagues by organising sack races instead of drill for the soldiers to exercise themselves. Two years later he ran for Parliament and was of course elected, though he only deigned to visit the House of Commons when not otherwise engaged.

Napoleon Bonaparte (1769-1821)

Some claim that the main reason he lost the battle of Waterloo was because he was suffering from haemorrhoids at the time and was thus unable to coordinate his troops from horseback.

Alfred Daniel Wintle (1897-1966)

This British colonel was so overbearing that when he was captured in France during the Second World War, he refused to eat until his guards smartened themselves up, cleaned their boots and promised to shave once a day. Surprisingly, they complied.

Charles Lindbergh (1902-74)

Not many people know that the U.S. aviator was a

Nazi apologist. In fact he once said that if America were to enter the Second World War, it should be on the side of the Germans.

Orde Wingate (1903-44)

Charterhouse-educated Wingate was a brilliant military strategist who rose quickly through the ranks of the army and whose campaigns in Palestine, Burma and Ethiopia made him into a military legend, He was also founder of the Chindits – a group of specially trained jungle fighters. Wingate was a complex character who had some strange ideas. He believed baths were unhealthy, and preferred to clean himself from top to toe with a brush – sometimes in the presence of visitors. The Israeli ambassador, Eliahu Elath witnessed this spectacle on one occasion.

He wore a tiny alarm clock on his little finger, which he programmed to go off at set times, abruptly breaking off important meetings when it did so, even if he was in mid-sentence. Considering his diet mainly consisted of raw onions, which he believed to be beneficial to his health, his colleagues were probably quite relieved by the interruption.

MISCELLANEOUS MADNESS

Simeon Ellerton

Ellerton was a Durham message-carrier who, on his return journeys from delivering messages, would pick up stones from the side of the road and bring them home in a bag on his head so that he could build himself a cottage out of them. After a few years he had enough and did so. After the cottage was built, however, he found he had spent so many years with big weights on his head that he found it strange to walk without them, so he continued going about the place to the end of his days with a heavy bag on his pate. When asked why he kept a bag of stones on his head he always gave the same answer: 'To keep my hat on'. It doesn't seem to have done him any harm either as he was deemed to be over a hundred years old when he died in 1799.

Sir Boyle Roche (1743-1807)

This Irish MP and chamberlain to the vice-regal court frequently got the sense of things mixed up when he was giving speeches. He was given to utterances like 'The cup of Ireland's miseries has been overflowing for centuries and is not yet full', and 'All along the untrodden paths of the future I see the footprints of an unseen hand'. He's also credited with being the originator of the phrase, 'What has posterity ever done for us?'

William Spooner (1844-1930)

This colourful Oxford lecturer is most famous for his confusion with words, often transposing the initial sounds of words e.g. 'You have hissed my mystery lectures'. He was also prone to absent-mindedness and once wrote a note asking a friend to visit him urgently, and then added a P.S. stating, 'I have dealt with the matter: please do not come'. On another occasion, he asked a man to come to dinner 'to meet Casson'. The man replied that he *was* Casson, and the indefatigable Will replied, 'Never mind, come all the same'.

At a wedding once he said it was 'kistomary to cuss the bride', and on another occasion informed a friend he was going to London on the 'town drain'. Even more abusively, he referred to Queen Victoria as 'The queer old dean', which might have been a more apt description of Dr Spooner himself.

Sir George Reresby Sitwell (1860-1943)

Antiquarian and genealogist, father of Edith and Osbert, this classic English eccentric once had his herd of white cows stencilled in a blue Chinese pattern to improve the prospect from the terrace at his family home, Renishaw Hall, in Derbyshire. Another time he was spotted crawling round the grounds on all fours, trying to work out how the lawn would look if he lowered it by a few feet.

Lord Berners (1883-1950)

Lord Gerald Hugh Tyrwhitt-Wilson, the 14th Baron Berners, was a man of many talents. He was a composer who collaborated with Stravinsky and Diaghilev, author of satirical novels and speaker of many languages. He was also a man of many eccentricities. He painted his doves bright colours and kitted his dogs out with diamond-studded collars. He had a harpsichord fitted into his Rolls-Royce so he could play as he was driven around the countryside by his chauffeur. He ensured privacy on trains by wearing dark glasses, reading his newspaper upside down and taking his temperature every five minutes. Anyone sharing his carriage soon became discomfited by this behaviour and sought another seat.

He also organised wild parties where the guests never knew what to expect – an explosion in the hall in the middle of the night, Berners dressed up in a grotesque mask appearing at their bedroom window, or waking up to find that the lawns had been transformed into a fairground.

Berners's biggest love was ballet (he composed several) as it was escapist art, providing a welcome relief from the troubles of the world. His many pranks and quirks can be seen as aiming at the same end. The epitaph he composed for himself ended 'Praise to the Lord / He never was bored!'.

Godfrey Hardy (1887-1947)

Hardy was one of Britain's finest mathematicians, but he was even more notable for his habit of watching cricket – his favourite hobby – with four or more layers of clothes on him. He called this his 'anti-God' apparel. His logic was that the Deity was malign if He existed at all and wouldn't get much pleasure out of causing it to rain while Hardy was protected against it. In this way he ensured the day would stay dry.

J.B.S. Haldane (1892-1965)

When this wilfully eccentric socialist and scientist of Scottish descent was asked if he believed in ESP, he said he thought it was 'a gross invasion of one's privacy'. He moved to India in 1957 because, he said, after 60 years he was fed up wearing socks (although it was actually in protest over the Suez crisis). He tried to get the 'No Smoking' signs in railway carriages replaced with ones saying 'No Perfume'.

William Strachey

The uncle of author Lytton Strachey spent five years in India in the 19th century. He believed so strongly that the only accurate clocks in the world were those in Calcutta that when he returned to England from that country he kept all the clocks and watches in his home at Calcutta time, which was six hours ahead of GMT. For 56 years afterwards he made it a practice to get up in the middle of the night, and go to bed at tea-time.

Sir Tatton Sykes

Nineteenth-century British aristocrat who had many behavioural quirks, one of which was a penchant for entering people's houses through the back door rather than the front. Consistent to a fault, he made his tenants enter their own houses in this manner as well.

Tony Hancock (1924-68)

The comedian used to bring the entire *Encyclopaedia Britannica* with him when he went on holiday. The set was as important a piece of baggage to him, according to one colleague, as his toothbrush.

Ruth van Herpen

This Dutch woman kissed a £17,000 painting by American artist Jo Baer in an Oxford Museum in 1977 'to cheer it up because it looked so sad'. A court ordered her to pay £1000 damages because her lipstick was ingrained in the canvas.

William Cheetey

Cheetey, an Ontario man, bought eight freezers in the 1960s, packing each one of them with three cubic feet of snow, a substance to which he was so attached he wanted to preserve it for posterity.

NAMES

William Randolph Hearst (1863-1951)

The publishing magnate once ordered that every one of his newspapers was to mention the name of his mistress Marion Davies at least once in every issue. The instruction was carried out for the next 30 years.

W.C. Fields (1880-1946)

Had hundreds of bank accounts held under a number of aliases to hide his assets from the taxman, or perhaps the women in his life. He opened accounts under such unlikely names as Figley Whiteside and Ludovic Fishpond in innumerable locations. Some of them may even still exist.

Brian Brown

Wolverhampton boxing fan who, in 1974, christened his daughter after every world heavyweight champion to date. She became Maria Sullivan Corbett Fitzsimmons Jeffries Hart Burns Johnson Willard Dempsey Tunney Schmeling Sharkey Carnero Baer Braddock Louis Charles Walcott Marciano Patterson Johannson Liston Clay Frazier Foreman Brown.

OBSESSIONS

Jonathan Swift (1667-1745)

Not only was he keen on exercise (see LITERARY LOONS), Swift was also obsessive about counting and once added up each step he took from his rooms in Chelsea to the centre of London, arriving at a final tally of 5748.

Samuel Johnson (1709-84)

The writer and lexicographer suffered from what we would now call Obsessive Compulsive Disorder, which resulted in the manic repetition of trivial actions. He made it a habit to touch every post he passed while walking. If he missed one, he had to go back to it. He also had a strange way of entering doors and passages: he had to go through each with a certain number of steps so that he always made the movement through the passage on the same foot. Otherwise he was miserable for the day.

Louis Francois de Bourbon (1717-1776)

The French politician was so chuffed about having made love to his wife 12 times in a single night that he subsequently had all his shirts marked with this number. He also bought 12 guns and 12 swords to mark the happy occasion. As if that wasn't enough, every time he went out he brought 12,000 francs with him. At home he made a routine of having 12 table settings for his guests and 12 courses for each dinner.

John Chapman (1774-1847)

Better known as Johnny Appleseed because of his obsession with apples, his obsession is reputed to have started shortly after he was born. In the cradle he cried non-stop if he wasn't given apples and as he grew he journeyed all round America planting apple seeds here, there and everywhere.

A kind and gentle man, he often offered seeds free of charge to those unable to afford to buy them, and also carried a Bible with him just in case anybody quoted him the Adam and Eve story as an apple deterrent. He strenuously pointed out that apples were never mentioned by name in the Good Book, the phrase in question being 'the fruit of the tree', which could have signified anything. He added that apples were mentioned favourably in the Bible no less than 11 times.

By 1838, Chapman had planted apple seeds in over 100,000 square miles of acreage, going barefoot for much of the time, and using red-hot irons to burn the wounds from his feet that resulted from his picaresque odysseys up hill and down dale. Nobody knows where his applemania originated from, but it lasted right up until the day he died.

Charles Stanhope (1780-1851)

Stanhope, the 4th Earl of Harrington, was so obsessed with snuff he had a different box for each day of the year. When a friend admired one that he was using, he replied that it was a nice summer box, but would not do for 'winter wear'.

Andrew McKellar

Eighteenth-century Scottish golfer who was so obsessed by the game that he played it in all weathers (snow simply entailed painting the ball red) and at all times of the day (when the sun went down he used a lamplight). Things reached a point where his wife eventually brought his dinner to him out on the course. Her action was meant to be a sardonic hint about her being a golf 'widow' but McKellar being McKellar imagined it was genuine and told her he would get to the meal as soon as he had finished his round.

H.L. Mencken (1880-1956)

The philologist, editor and satirist often washed his hands up to a dozen times an hour for fear of picking up germs.

Fred Astaire (1899-1987)

Was obsessed with soap operas, so much so that when work commitments precluded him watching them he made frantic calls to his housemaid to find out plot developments.

Alfred Hitchcock (1899-1980)

As a boy Hitchcock was obsessed with maps and train timetables, and one of his hobbies was memorising them: at one stage he knew nearly all of the timetables in Britain. Traces of obsession, which according to one commentator 'appealed to the part of him that liked everything regulated and on schedule', can be seen in his films such as *The Lady Vanishes* and *North by Northwest*.

Henry Cope

The 19th-century dandy known as The Green Man of Brighton because of his green pantaloons, green waistcoat, green frock coat and green cravat, ate only green fruits and vegetables and had his room and furniture painted green too.

Walt Disney (1901-66)

The creator of Mickey Mouse was so addicted to handwashing he cleaned them up to 30 times an hour.

Howard Hughes (1905-76)

He had a well-documented obsession with germs, wrapping every piece of furniture in either crepe paper or Kleenex. His staff were prohibited from touching anything, however innocuous. If they opened a can of food for him, no part of their body was allowed to be over the can and their heads had to be kept at a 45-degree angle from it. If they coughed as it was being opened it had to be thrown away. Neither were they allowed to talk to him, having to merely nod their heads in response to instructions from him. They were also forbidden to use fly-swatters for fear their movements would recycle germs lying dormant in the air-conditioning system. He had a particular fear of flies and went into a panic if one flew into his room. This was an unusual occurrence anyway, considering he had his windows and doors hermetically sealed.

Tony Hancock (1924-68)

Fascinated by Punch and Judy shows since childhood, Hancock was obsessed with puppets of all sorts and felt they could control his life. When he was working with a ventriloquist in 1951 he spoke to his dummy as if it were a real person. Even if it was hanging from a coat-hook in his dressing room he felt it was watching him accusingly. He had nightmares about it which caused him to wake up in a cold sweat, screaming. When Hancock was working with the ventriloquist he insisted the dummy be present even during rehearsals and for radio shows, and not just when they were appearing before a live audience. 'I can't make the words live unless he's here,' he claimed.

Andy Warhol (1928-87)

The artist was so fascinated by Truman Capote when he first went to New York that he used to stand outside his house at all hours of the day and night waiting for him to come out. He pestered him with so many phone calls, Capote's mother eventually had to warn him to desist.

Jayne Mansfield (1933-67)

The actress was so obsessed with pink that she had everything in her house painted in the colour. She also bathed in pink champagne.

David Lynch (1946-)

The quirky director of 'Twin Peaks' ordered the very same meal at the same time at a diner for seven years.

Howdy Giles

American dentist who was so obsessed with golfer Arnold Palmer he ended up wearing only clothes endorsed by him. He also put his image on his personalised stationery and swapped his car for a Cadillac from a Palmer dealership. Finally, he bought a condominium next door to Palmer's Bay Hill home so he could watch him practice. Palmer was more flattered than threatened by such adulation and in 1977 made him his official dentist. Shortly afterwards, Giles removed a number of gold fillings from Palmer's mouth and melted them down to make a ball marker for himself.

José Moura

José, a Brazilian, is obsessed with kissing celebrities. He was once dragged off a tennis court after trying to kiss Martina Navratilova when she was playing a match against Monica Seles. When the Pope visited Rio de Janeiro in 1980, José couldn't get near the pontiff's face so settled for kissing his feet instead.

Neil Gordon Wilson

Had an obsession with being a fish, and when his dead body was found in Victoria, Australia in 1995 he was dressed from head to toe in a fish suit made from water bed plastic. It had round holes for the eyes but no other kind of ventilation, which made the state pathologist wonder how he managed to breathe inside it for as long as he did. Locals later confided that he had spent most of his free time floating on a lake, supported by a rope that hung from a tree overhead.

PERSEVERANCE

Cardinal Richelieu (1585-1642)

Despite ill-health in his final years, this French prelate and statesman continued to travel, having his servants carry him through the streets in his bed, and ordering them to break down walls if the places he wished to stay in had entrances that were too narrow for it to go through.

Sir Isaac Newton (1642-1727)

At one point of his life, Newton was Professor of Mathematics at Cambridge University, but his lectures went way above the heads of his pupils so they eventually stopped turning up. Newton didn't, and continued to appear at the lecture hall week after week at the appointed time, delivering his lectures to the empty desks.

John Pierpoint Morgan (1837-1913)

Enterprising American millionaire who bet a friend $10,000 in 1907 that a man could walk round the world without his face being seen. He employed playboy Harry Bensley to try it out, wearing an iron mask. Bensley was only allowed £1 spending money and had to push a pram as he went on his travels. He had no clothes except what he wore and a change of underwear. He set out from Trafalgar Square and spent the next six years pushing his pram across 12 countries, passing through Sydney, Montreal and New York on his travels. In August 1914 he arrived in Genoa, having only six more countries to visit, but the First World War made this impossible. He received over 200 offers of marriage during his picaresque existence, but declined them all.

Juan Potomachi

Buenos Aires businessman who died in 1955, leaving 200,000 pesos to a fund for trainee actors on the condition that his head be preserved and used as a skull for a production of *Hamlet*. Juan had been a failed actor himself and this was his last gasp effort to tread the boards, albeit posthumously and minus his torso.

Les Stewart

An Australian who suffered horrific burns in a housefire and found himself only able to type with one finger. He lost his job but instead of remaining idle he decided to type out all the numbers from one to a million. He typed for 20 minutes every hour and after 16 years and seven months he had completed his task. It took him seven typewriters, 1000 ink ribbons and 19,900 sheets of paper. He is now in the *Guinness Book of Records* as winner of the world's longest typewriter marathon.

Derek Wadlow

This Middlesex eccentric shortened 300,000 matches by an inch in 1980 so that they would fit into smaller boxes than the ones in which he bought them. In later years he took it upon himself to perform other interesting tasks, such as giftwrapping 1400 coconuts and putting 11,400 live earthworms into 1900 plastic bags.

PHYSIOLOGY

Tycho Brahe (1546-1601)

The royal Danish astronomer had his nose sliced off in a swordfight whereupon he ordered surgeons to clamp a specially designed golden one on him instead, using money that had been given to him for research by the King of Denmark. In his pocket he carried a box of glue to strengthen it whenever it became loose.

Samuel Pepys (1663-1703)

The writer kept the skin on his face smooth by rubbing it repeatedly with a pumice stone.

George Washington (1732-99)

Having lost virtually all his teeth before he became President, he had a set of dentures made from cow's teeth, and another from the tusks of a hippo. They were hinged together and opened and shut on springs.

Marie Louise

This redoubtable lady, who was Napoleon's second wife, was able to move her ears at will, and even turn them inside out.

Duke of Wellington (1769-1852)

A vestigial tail growing from the base of his spine meant that the Duke could only ride on horseback using a specially adapted saddle with a hole at the rear.

Hans Christian Andersen (1805-75)

The writer was so thin he stuffed his shirt with paper every morning before leaving the house to make himself look more chunky.

Clarence Willard

Willard was a performance artist born in Ohio in 1882 who was able to make himself taller or smaller by stretching his muscles to inordinate lengths. A tailor's nightmare, he had great fun at their expense whenever he went to be measured for suits, adept at fabricating deformities at will and then reverting back to normal size when his garments had already been cut. He made a living from this quirky talent, appearing on stage beside people who started by looking taller than him and ended diminutive by comparison. During one of his shows he extended his height from 5 feet 10 inches to an incredible 6 feet 4 inches.

Ben Turpin (1874-1940)

Comic star of the silent screen, Turpin had an insurance policy with Lloyds of London for £100,000 to protect his famous crossed eyes from becoming normal.

E.M. Forster (1879-1970)

The author was so short-sighted he once bowed in front of a cake, imagining it to be a member of the Royal Family.

Rupert Brooke (1887-1915)

The poet could pick up a ball with his foot as he had prehensile toes. He could also hold a matchbox with one foot and strike a match off it with the other one.

King Carol II (1893-1953)

Romanian ruler whose penis was reputed to be so large, operations had to be performed on a huge number of women in his harem in order to be able to receive it. Some of them were rumoured to have died when their perinea ruptured after sex with him.

Carl Herman Unthan

Armless 19th-century Prussian who was able to wash, dress, sharpen pencils and use a knife and fork with his feet. When he was 12 he tied a violin to a stool, picked up the bow with his feet and started to play. He later became famous as a concert artist, drawing praise from such august listeners as Franz Liszt.

Bing Crosby (1904-77)

The singer used to pin his cauliflower ears back with spirit gum.

POLITICS

Caligula (AD12-41)

The Roman emperor was so disenchanted with the political acumen of his colleagues that he considered appointing his horse a consul.

Benjamin Franklin (1706-90)

Liked to walk around naked even into his eighties, which sometimes sent housemaids screaming in terror as he nonchalantly came into view. He called these nude perambulations 'air baths' and thought they gave him inspiration for his writing.

George Washington (1732-99)

The first President of the United States used to carry a sundial round with him instead of a watch to tell the time. He also grew marijuana in his garden. When he met people on the street, he used to bow to them rather than shake their hands, because he thought shaking hands was undignified.

William Harrison (1773-1841)

Despite the fact that the weather was freezing and rainy, he refused to wear an overcoat at his inauguration as U.S. President in 1841, preferring to be seen in his well-cut suit. He got pneumonia as a result of his sartorial stubbornness and died 30 days later, making his the shortest presidency in American history.

Zachary Taylor (1784-1850)

This war hero never voted in an election in his life but went on to become the 12th president of the U.S. Taylor was late in acknowledging his nomination for the presidency because the letter informing him it had come through had no stamp on it and he refused to pay the postman. He held office for half a day before gorging himself on pastries and corn whiskey, subsequently passing out for 84 hours.

Abraham Lincoln (1809-65)

Lincoln failed in business at the age of 22 and the following year lost a bid for the legislature. At 24 he failed in business again and at 26 his girlfriend died. At 27 he had a nervous breakdown and at 29 was defeated for the post of Speaker of the House in the State Legislature. At 34 he ran for Congress and lost, and again at 39. At age 46 he ran for the U.S. Senate and lost. At 47 he ran for Vice-President and lost too. Lincoln was 51 when he became President of the U.S.

Calvin Coolidge (1872-1933)

The U.S. President often used to jump into bushes to fool his bodyguards, then jump out and give them a fright.

Winston Churchill (1874-1965)

Frequent bouts of depression gave Churchill suicidal leanings. He often felt the urge to throw himself off railway platforms or over the sides of boats.

Herbert Hoover (1874-1964)

The U.S. president was so cautious about public pronouncements that when he was on a train journey with a friend who commented that the sheep in a nearby field had been sheared, Hoover thought for a moment and then murmured gingerly, 'Yes – at least on this side'.

Joseph Stalin (1879-1953)

Long before his dictatorship (which resulted in the deaths of over 20 million people) Stalin trained to be a Priest at the Tiflis Theological Seminary in Georgia. He was expelled eventually for spreading Marxist propaganda.

Adolf Hitler (1889-1945)

A recent biography written with the assistance of his former bodyguards reveals that he had a secret fantasy of being a cowboy, which he acted out on country walks, crouching down behind trees and bushes and firing a loaded pistol at imaginary Indians surrounding him. He loved reading about life in the Wild West so much he set up a special museum in honour of his favourite author Karl May, who wrote tales about North American Indians, in 1928. More than seven million people have visited the museum (located in Dresden) since then.

J. Edgar Hoover (1895-1972)

Hoover was arrested for soliciting boys in New Orleans in the late 1920s, a fact known to the Mafia, which meant he was in their pocket for most of his FBI career and thus powerless to do anything against them.

Gerald Ford (1913-)

The 38th president of the United States was a male model before he went into politics.

Idi Amin (1925-)

The Ugandan soldier and dictator sent Richard Nixon a card in 1973 wishing him a 'speedy recovery' from Watergate.

George Smathers

Politician who won the 1950 U.S. Senate primary elections in Florida by exploiting the voting public, who ranked him low in the linguistics department. He said of his opponent Claude Pepper, 'He went in for celibacy before marriage', was 'a practising *homo sapiens*', and that he had a sister who was a 'thespian'. His verbal tricks earned him the nomination.

PRANKSTERS

Timothy Dexter (1747-1806)

American self-made man who arranged a mock funeral for himself to see how many people would turn up. He then interrupted the proceedings in full flow in his baronial mansion, almost causing the assembled 3000 guests apoplexy. His wife wasn't

weeping as much as he'd hoped so he throttled her.
His action produced the requisite tears, albeit for all
the wrong reasons.

7th Earl of Barrymore (1769-1793)

This Regency aristocrat (nicknamed 'Hellgate') was
addicted to practical jokes, his favourite of which was
putting coffins, containing servants made up to look
like corpses, in a vertical position outside people's
doors with the lid open and then ringing the bell.
When he went on picnics he made the servants hide
the food, which his guests then had to search for.

Theodore Hook (1788-1841)

English playwright and celebrated practical joker,
Hook is most famous for the Berners Street hoax of
1809. He was walking through this street with the
playwright Samuel Beazley, who commented on its
quietness. Hook bet him a guinea that within a week
he would have everyone in London talking about it. A
week later, Beazley and Hook took a room in a
lodging house and watched hundreds of people turn
up to No. 54. The congregation included: 12 chimney
sweeps; 20 coal-laden wagons; cartloads of furniture;
a hearse; coachmakers; clockmakers; wigmakers;
opticians and tradespeople. Hook had ordered all of
them. Not only that, he had placed an advertisement for
domestic staff and there were many hopefuls on the
doorstep. Hearst had also written to a variety of
dignitaries, informing them that Mrs Tottenham, the

woman who actually lived at No. 54, was about to dispose of her vast wealth. The Lord Mayor of London, the Archbishop of Canterbury, the Governor of the Bank of England and the Lord Chief Justice accordingly turned up. And finally, the Duke of York arrived with his cavalry as he had been told his mistress was dying there. Pandemonium broke out in the street and Hook won his guinea.

Herbert Spencer (1820-1903)

The English philosopher and evolutionist precursor of Darwin, Spencer is remembered today chiefly for coining the phrase 'survival of the fittest'. An odd person in his private life, he refused to travel anywhere without a hammock, hanging it in train compartments in preference to sitting on the hard seats provided. He was also a practical joker, and once nearly drove a colleague out of his mind by adding a strip of paper inside his hatband each day to make him think his head was growing in size.

Sir Herbert Draper Beerbohm Tree (1853-1917)

Once went into a posh lady's garden and took off all the labels on her roses, replacing their Italian names with those of (in)famous criminals such as Dr Crippen.

H.L. Mencken (1880-1956)

Wrote an apocryphal article in the *New York Evening Mail* in 1917 complaining about the fact that nobody had celebrated the 75th anniversary of the introduction of the bathtub into the U.S. A man named Adam Thompson, he alleged, had been responsible for its installation, performing the gallant deed in the face of staunch disapprovers, who saw it as 'an obnoxious toy designed to corrupt democratic simplicity'. Its subsequent history, the article went on to state, was rather traumatic. Tubs were subjected to tax levies in Virginia, permitted only on prescription in Boston and banned outright in some other states for health reasons. All this was taken as gospel by a nation of gullible readers. The piece created quite a stir, and was reprinted in many other newspapers of the time, so Mencken eventually had to admit he made it all up for a bit of fun to cheer people up amid the depression of the First World War.

William Horace de Vere Cole (1881-1936)

The London poet-cum-painter and trickster sent four bald friends of his to a play he hated. When they took off their respective hats as it started, the audience hooted as it saw the letters S, H, I and T painted on their pates. Another time he invited a group of people to a reception, all of whose names ended in 'Bottom'. He didn't go himself, merely enjoyed imagining the reaction when Mr Ramsbottom met Mr Shufflebottom, and Mr Higginbottom met Mr Winterbottom. On a third occasion he asked a stranger on the street to hold one end of a ball of twine, pretending he was measuring a distance. He disappeared round a corner and handed the other end of the twine to another stranger, telling him the same lie. Then he disappeared leaving them to unravel the mystery.

One afternoon Cole came across a road crew without a foreman in London. He took it upon himself to fill the vacancy and directed the men to Piccadilly Circus. A policeman diverted the traffic for the workers, and it was several hours before the city noticed the unauthorised hole they had dug in the street.

The most well-known of his pranks is the 'Dreadnought' hoax of 1910. Cole rang Mr Cholmondeley from the Foreign Office and told him that the Emperor of Abyssinia would be visiting England. A ceremonial guard met Cole and five friends (including a young Virginia Woolf), dressed up as the Emperor and his entourage, and speaking in a language they were making up as they went along.

Robert Benchley (1889-1945)

The American writer tried to visit the enclosed tomb of Ulysses S. Grant in New York but found the door locked. Being the mischief-maker he was, he reached into his pocket for pen and paper, started writing furiously and then slipped the note under the door. The next morning the janitor picked it up to read the words: 'Please leave 2 quarts Grade A and 1 pint of whipping cream. U.S.G.'

Stan Laurel (1890-1965)

Simulated epileptic fits at dinner parties by placing Alka-Seltzer tablets under his tongue and spitting them out as if they were foam. He once pretended to be choking to death after a meal, 'throwing up' food he had hidden in a hot water bottle he kept under his jacket.

Billy Buttress

The 19th-century ventriloquist would mime a cat's miaows, receiving much pleasure from watching fellow travellers search desperately for the feline, laughing when they found only his dummy – a stuffed cat.

Lou Stone

Nineteenth-century American journalist who wrote the most ridiculous stories in print history but somehow managed to make them seem credible. In his capacity as cub reporter for the *Evening Standard* in Connecticut he covered topics such as trees that had baked apples on their branches, cows that produced ice-cream instead of milk, rivers that ran uphill, cats that whistled 'Yankee Doodle Dandy', a farmer who kept flies away by painting a picture of a spider on his bald head, and a hen that, on the 4th of July, laid eggs that were coloured red, white and blue.

Graham Greene (1904-91)

Had a dotty habit of looking through the phone book for other Graham Greenes and then ringing them up to give out stink about the pornography in 'their' books. One particular individual eventually had to go ex-directory, so haunted was he by repeated crank calls from the mischievous scribe, all made in different voices Greene put on to disguise himself.

Salvador Dali (1904-89)

Dali once arrived at a surrealist exhibition in 1936 with a billiard cue in one hand, two Russian wolfhounds on a leash in the other, and a scuba diving suit wrapped round him. It was intended to be a prank, but he was so tightly enclosed inside it he almost suffocated. He screamed out, but he also had a tight helmet on so nobody heard him. It was only after he made frantic gestures with his hands that people realised he was in trouble. A caretaker released him finally – with a screwdriver.

Lewis Carroll (1932-98)

The author often called for children by ringing their doorbell, then going down on all fours and barking through the letterbox.

Joe Orton (1933-67)

The playwright was fond of practical jokes and used to write spoof letters haranguing various bodies and people under the name of Edna Welthorpe, including one to a vicar asking if she could stage a play about gays in the church hall. Another missive went to the Home Shopping Service saying that she had tried Smedley's raspberry pie filling only to find that there was no raspberry in it, much to her chagrin. The demented Ms Welthorpe also wrote a stern letter to Crosse and Blackwell complaining about the fact that a tin of blackberry pie filling had almost poisoned her Aunt Lydia. She sent another one to the Ritz Hotel claiming she had left her Moroccan leather handbag in the lounge, containing snaps of herself in the nude, and she wanted it back immediately. The Ritz weren't able to help, but Crosse and Blackwell sent her a case of blackberry pie filling cans for her pains.

In 1962 Orton was convicted of stealing and defacing over 70 library books, often returning them secretly to the library afterwards and watching browsers' bemused reactions as they scanned them. He superimposed a picture of a nude woman on the cover of an etiquette book. He also typed false blurbs on the back flaps of books, some of which were obscene. The typeface on his typewriter led to his detection and he was fined £200 alongside his partner-in-crime Kenneth Halliwell and they both served six months. The sentence would have been greater had not their probation officer described the pair of them as frustrated authors desperately searching for some way to get themselves into print.

Alasdair Gray (1934-)

The Scottish novelist, fond of practical jokes, once had his publishers put an erratum slip in the first edition of a novel of his which read 'this erratum slip has been inserted by mistake'.

Edward Lindley Wood

Wood, the Earl of Halifax and Britain's Foreign Secretary during the Second World War, had a wicked sense of humour. Travelling on a train one day he found himself sitting opposite two rather prim-looking ladies and decided to have a joke at their expense. When the train went into a tunnel he started to jump around in his seat, making smooching noises by kissing his hand. When the train came out of the tunnel he looked at them and asked, 'To which of you two ladies am I indebted to for those passionate moments?' Thoroughly unsuspecting of the hoax, they looked daggers at one another as he tittered to himself.

RECLUSES

Charles Seymour (1662-1748)

Seymour, the 6th Duke of Somerset, was a decidedly odd 17th-century figure. He refused to communicate with his servants except in sign language and he built houses along the way to London to save himself the indignity of staying at inns *en route*. He took a nap after dinner each day and delegated his daughter Charlotte to watch over him lest he fall off his couch. One day she wandered outside and he fell off it. To punish her for her sins he refused to speak to her for a year.

Henry Cavendish (1731-1810)

Eighteenth-century philosopher who was so snobbish that when he passed one of his maids on the stairs of his house one day, he made a point of having a second staircase installed so that the embarrassing event wouldn't happen again. He rarely left his house and was so bashful he even left notes for his cook regarding his meals to avoid having to speak to him.

William Beckford (1760-1844)

Beckford began life as a wealthy man and was a writer, a friend of Voltaire and a collector of the arts. His downfall began when he went into exile in 1784, after being caught buggering a boy eight years his junior, sodomy being a capital offence. When he returned in 1820 he became a recluse, throwing all his energies into creating buildings on his Wiltshire estate which was surrounded by high walls and spiked railings. Here Beckford lived alone but for a troup of homosexual servants and a dwarf whose diet consisted of mushrooms. On certain occasions he got so bored he would deliberately throw himself from his horse into a nearby lake in the hope that he would be drowned.

William Bentinck-Scott (1800-49)

Bentinck-Scott was the 5th Duke of Portland and an MP from 1824 to 1826. He presided over a sprawling estate manned by a huge number of labourers, none of whom were allowed to speak to him or else they would be sacked on the spot. As well as improving his lavish Nottinghamshire domain, he also had them install an underground railway that ran from his house to a ballroom some distance away. (The ballroom was never used, nor were the vast stables William built on a similar whim.) The railway ran through 15 miles of tunnels, achieving the desired purpose. When he had to travel outside his estate, however, other stratagems for anonymity had to be employed, so he had a coach built that had especially low seats and impenetrable blinds to stop people gawking in at him. He also wore masses of clothes to disguise himself, as well as a false beard and moustache, and a hat that was almost two feet high.

Ferociously reclusive, he didn't even allow his doctor to take his temperature when he was sick, making him stand outside his door instead and pass the thermometer to him by means of his valet as he called his symptoms out through the door.

Florence Nightingale (1820-1910)

Dined almost every day for five years with Sydney Herbert, one of her colleagues in hospital reform. When Herbert died from kidney failure in 1861 she was so traumatised she said, 'He takes my life with him. Why did God not set aside a few trifling physical laws to save him?'

She became a total recluse in the aftermath of his demise, locking herself in her room and refusing to speak to anyone. She even cancelled her newspaper for fear she'd read of the death of someone else she was close to. She lived for 50 more years, continuing her work from her home but seeing people (such as the Aga Khan and General Gordon) by appointment only. Visitors to her were, upon arrival, given a pencil and a piece of paper with which to state their business and this was then brought upstairs to her by a member of her staff. She usually refused to see them. Even the Queen of Holland was rebuffed. ('She is the queen of queens, but it is quite, quite, quite impossible.') Some people tried to speak to her through her keyhole but she didn't reply, busy answering her correspondence from a sofa upstairs which she shared with her many cats.

Emily Dickinson (1830-86)

The poet never left home from the age of 30 to her death. On the odd occasions that she had visitors she spoke to them from behind a wall because she was so self-conscious about her appearance. She dressed only in white. Dickinson wrote nearly 2000 poems which she stuffed in cupboards or embroidered on cushions; they were discovered only after she died.

Marcel Proust (1871-1922)

Had the walls of his room cork-lined so he could write without fear of external noise. So obsessed was he with privacy, he used to buy up the houses that surrounded his and leave them empty.

P.G. Wodehouse (1881-1975)

Was so painfully shy that when he was staying in apartment complexes he always tried to find rooms on the ground floor because he was useless at making smalltalk with elevator operators. He used to laugh loudly on country walks as ideas for books came to him, but if there was anybody nearby he would dart behind a tree and hide there from embarrassment until they passed. At a party given by his wife Ethel, he met guests at the door with the line, 'Don't go in: you won't enjoy it'. On a subsequent occasion, to get out of attending a function, he told a female journalist he was going to Georgia. It was a lie, but to cover himself he actually went!

Langley Collyer (1885-1947)

Langley and his brother Homer totally cut themselves off from New York society after their parents separated in 1909. They lived with their mother for the next 20 years and when she died they spent most of their time inside the walls of their three-storey mansion in Harlem collecting objects such as books, bicycles, sewing machines, scrap iron and the like. Many people thought they were millionaires even though Langley was often seen foraging in garbage cans for food.

When they stopped paying their water and electricity bills, they took to cooking meals on a small kerosene stove and getting water from a park fountain four blocks away. In 1933 Homer went blind and Langley convinced himself he could cure him by having him eat a hundred oranges a week. Alas, this didn't work, and seven years later he became paralysed as well. By now Langley had barricaded all the doors and windows with debris to keep intruders out, and he also installed ingenious booby traps.

One such trap was to have ironic reverberations in 1947, however, for it fell on top of him that year, crushing him to death as he was on his way to Homer with some food. Homer died of starvation not long afterwards, which meant that the sight that greeted the police when they eventually broke the doors down wasn't pretty. As well as the two bodies they found over 120 tons of the materials they had been collecting all their lives: not only the books, bicycles and sewing machines but also barbed wire, tree limbs, obscene photographs, the jawbone of a horse, 14 grand pianos and even the chassis of a model-T Ford.

James Lucas

Lucas, the 'Mad Hermit of Hertfordshire', was a thoroughly weird 19th-century figure who withdrew into himself unconditionally after his mother died. He refused to bury her, embalming her instead and keeping her in a glass coffin in his drawing-room. The police eventually broke in and took her corpse away after 13 weeks and after this point James turned his house into a veritable fortress. A horse-rug was his only mode of dress and he neither washed nor groomed himself for years. Charles Dickens visited him once but after a brief altercation Lucas sent him packing - with the help of a shotgun. Afterwards he employed bodyguards to keep others away, though he sometimes gave sweets to children who gazed fascinated at this straggly character sitting in his sackcloth behind barred windows.

John Slater

This erratic 20th-century Scot currently lives in a cave, unperturbed by the fact that it gets flooded at high tide. He was once married, but spent so much time in the cave that his wife told him to choose – her or it. He eventually chose the latter option. Afterwards he walked from Land's End to John O'Groats in his pyjamas. He was also shoeless, but for company he brought his dog with him, which enjoyed the luxury of suede bootees. Slater once volunteered to spend six months in London Zoo in a cage as a human exhibit to raise money for the preservation of the panda. The Zoo declined the offer.

Samuel Beckett (1906-89)

Literature's archetypal recluse, Beckett hated leaving his house even to buy a stamp and was known to have spent hours in people's company without uttering a word.

Robert Redford (1937-)

The actor books whole rows of seats on airplanes so that he won't have to speak to anybody else on the journey.

REINCARNATION

Prince de Condé

Eighteenth-century French nobleman who expended great energy building luxurious stables for his horses at Chantilly because he believed he was going to be reincarnated as a horse ... hopefully in Chantilly.

Sir Arthur Conan Doyle (1859-1930)

The creator of Sherlock Holmes was a spiritualist and predicted his resurrection would take place ten days after his death in the Albert Hall. Ten thousand people turned up in July 1930 to witness the resurrection, but dispersed after there was no sign of Doyle's return.

George Patton (1885-1945)

This general believed he had six previous incarnations, including a Napoleonic marshal, an English knight, a prehistoric warrior, a soldier of Alexander the Great and a legionnaire with Julius Caesar in Northern Gaul.

Andy Warhol (1928-87)

The artist didn't want an epitaph or even his name on his tombstone, just the word 'Figment'. He wanted to be reincarnated as a ring on Liz Taylor's finger.

Ada Stewart (1929-)

This Scottish lady believed she was the reincarnation of her fellow countryman James IV. One night in 1967 she claimed to have re-experienced the Battle of Flodden where James fought the English in 1513. She woke up screaming, telling everybody that she had been taken over by his personality. In 1970 she wrote a book called *The Autobiography of James IV, King of Scots*. Asked for her biological details she replied tartly. 'Died 1513: Born 1929.'

Arthur Robby

American farmer who launched a campaign against fish-eating in 1959, believing Jesus was going to be reincarnated as a mackerel.

RELIGION

St Augustine (354-430)

Abstained from sex all his life because sperm came from the same organ that produces urine.

St Kevin

This 6th-century Irish hermit lived in a cave in Wicklow, spending half of his time praying and the other half, if we're to believe the legend, fending off the advances of a woman called Kathleen who tried to wean him away from the path of righteousness. He punished himself by stripping naked and lying down in a bed of nettles but when Kathleen discovered his hiding place he used the nettles to punish her instead. He eventually decided she was the devil and pushed her into a nearby lake.

St Bernard (1090-1153)

Once excommunicated a swarm of flies for buzzing too loudly while he was preaching.

John Bunyan (1628-88)

The author of *The Pilgrim's Progress* renounced hockey for life after a vision appeared to him one Sunday which he took to be a message from heaven.

Elspeth Buchan

Born near Glasgow in 1738, Elspeth interpreted the Bible literally, becoming something of a religious nut in time. She proclaimed herself to be the lady described in the Book of Revelation where it says, 'There appeared a wonder in heaven: a woman clothed with the sun, and the moon under her feet, and upon her head a crown of twelve stars'. Like many fanatics, she acquired a large following for her organisation, the 'Buchan Society'. If members decided they'd had enough and wished to leave it, she ordered them either to be locked up or ducked in cold water – or both.

One day she informed her members that they would all ascend to heaven the following morning, and that they were to throw away all their material possessions to accelerate the momentous event. When the day dawned, however, and the expectant horde remained firmly attached to the ground, she lost her rag and turned on them, castigating them for not having enough faith. It was this and this alone, she contended, that was responsible for the ascension not taking place. To make it happen, she declared, they must all fast for 40 days and 40 nights, which would make them light enough to levitate to celestial regions. Some of them were mad enough to attempt this but when they came close to death from starvation the fast was abandoned, much to Elspeth's chagrin. She herself, conveniently enough, didn't go on the fast.

When she was dying, she told her disciples that she was only departing the earth for a short time. She would make a plea for them all to get into heaven with her when she got there, she announced, and would return to collect them after six months. If they didn't believe this, however, she wouldn't come back for ten years. If ten years elapsed and they still weren't convinced she was coming back for them, she would delay her return for a further 40 years. It didn't seem to occur to her that most of them would themselves have departed this earth by then.

William Miller (1782-1849)

Self-styled American prophet of doom who prophesied that the world would come to an end on April 3 1843, causing some religious fanatics to commit suicide because they believed that the first dead would be the first to get to heaven. His disciples convened on a large hill in New England on the day in question, some of them dressed in ascension robes and some naked. A blaring noise rang out in Vermont, but all it turned out to be was a village idiot blowing his horn. Another man wearing turkey wings attached to his shoulders broke his arm trying to fly heavenwards when the clouds failed to part.

Miller was undaunted, however, and re-set the Armageddon date for March 21 of the following year.

Again this day came and passed without a mushroom cloud or fireball. Miller now admitted he'd miscalculated and that the real day of destruction would be October 22. This time the numbers were depleted, but there were still some die-hards (if that's not the wrong expression in the circumstances). One man, a farmer, even brought his cows along, reasoning very wisely that it was a long way to heaven and 'the kids will want milk.' Alas, nothing happened again. The good old world continued to turn and the remaining trickle of Millerites disbanded. William himself passed into obscurity as he went back to farming, using his old ascension robes to keep his cows warm in winter.

Archbishop Richard Whateley (1787-1863)

The Protestant Archbishop of Dublin, author of several books, had many mannerisms that more befitted a fidgety juvenile than an esteemed man of the cloth. He climbed trees for fun even in his middle years, often swinging from the branches for exercise. In people's houses he swayed incessantly in chairs, frequently causing them to break into smithereens with his exertions – he broke six belonging to one acquaintance alone.

He also had a habit of contorting himself: raising his right leg, doubling it back over the thigh of the left one, and then grabbing his instep with his hands and tugging it as though his foot were some small animal that he was trying to strangle. And he was even known to put his foot in someone's pocket at a Privy Council meeting.

Sylvester Graham (1794-1851)

This Presbyterian minister believed that bakers laced their bread with pipe clay, chalk and even plaster of Paris, thereby making it highly injurious to one's health. He waged such a war on bread in Boston in the 1840s that a lynch mob of bakers stormed his hotel in 1847, intent on stringing him up to the nearest tree for damaging their trade.

Rev. John Alington (1795-1863)

The British rector, known as 'Mad Jack', inherited an enormous manor house and 43 farms in Hertfordshire from his grandfather. He then replaced his father as a preacher at the parish church, but was suspended from office because he gave sermons on the pleasures of free love. Undaunted, he preached from a pulpit in Letchworth Hall, enticing the audience away from his replacement with free beer and brandy. Sometimes his congregation grew so rowdy he had to threaten them with a shotgun.

He also believed it was his responsibility to educate the people who worked on his estate. To that end he turned a pond on his land into a scale model of the world: his workers rowed him round the various 'countries' as he taught them all about them.

George Henry (1801-88)

The New Yorker believed that to truly praise the Lord one had to be exuberant, laughing, shouting and leaping about the church as one expressed one's adoration. Such antics were infectious and his services attracted hundreds of enthusiasts who joined in the fun. George went blind in old age but that didn't stop his shenanigans.

He also wrote a book which has the longest title in literary history. It was called: *Shouting, Genuine And Spurious, In All Ages Of The Church, From The Birth Of Creation, When The Sons Of God Shouted For Joy, Until The Shout Of The Archangel: With Numerous Extracts From The Old And New Testaments, And From The Works of Wesley, Evans, Edwards, Abbott, Cartwright And Finley, Giving A History Of The Outward Demonstrations Of The Spirit, Such As Laughing, Screaming, Shouting, Leaping, Jerking And Falling Under The Power.*

Victor Hugo (1802-85)

The French author claimed to have discussed theology with Jesus at séances.

John Humphrey Noyes (1811-86)

When Noyes was rejected for ordination as a preacher in the Congregational church in the U.S. in the 1840s, he set up his own 'Perfectionist' church which held that true love meant sharing one's body with whomsoever one pleased. He founded a community where free love was on offer to all and sundry, married or not, but he didn't use this phrase, preferring to call it 'complex marriage', which sounded more lofty. Three hundred people joined his community, changing partners as they saw fit, but without obligation to 'perform' if they felt uneasy about doing so. In 1847 he was arrested for adultery but jumped bail and reunited with his followers. He had hundreds of lovers but was charged with statutory rape in 1877. All of this he took in his stride, stating that he firmly believed in the perfectibility of humankind through what he called 'Bible Communism': a convenient phrase that, translated into English, seemed to mean free love.

Robert Louis Stevenson (1850-94)

The author once attempted to convert a flock of sheep to Calvinism by reading The Bible aloud to them.

Adolf Hitler (1889-1945)

At one stage of his life Hitler contemplated becoming a priest. He used to stand on a kitchen chair in his house and put an apron over his shoulders as he delivered what passed for sermons to his parents.

Aimee McPherson (1890-1944)

Canadian evangelist who drew huge crowds with her born-again homilies and pentecostal exuberance. She dressed ostentatiously and behaved accordingly, on one occasion putting on a policeman's uniform and riding a motorbike down the aisle of a church to drive her point home. She was married three times, but none of her husbands could satisfy her fiery personality or her penchant for kinky sex: sometimes performed with candles and crucifixes as backdrops.

Robert Hawker

Nineteenth-century English poet and rector who preached in a Cornish parish and always wore a fisherman's jersey and sea boots under his clerical gear and spent much of his time in Cornwall in a cliff-top hut smoking opium. He once excommunicated a cat for catching a mouse on the Sabbath.

Edward Hine

Nineteenth-century stockbroker-turned-author from London who believed fervently that his fellow Brits comprised the ten lost tribes of Israel. He prophesied their imminent return to the Holy Land, an event that would be followed by the Second Coming of Christ. After Queen Victoria had read some of his tomes she remarked, 'If and when his prophecies come true, I'll gladly transfer my government to Palestine.'

Oric Bovar (1917-77)

New York cult leader who announced in 1970 that he was Jesus Christ, and that henceforth Christmas was to be celebrated on his own birthday, August 29th, instead of December 25th. His devotees were only too happy to oblige, but shortly afterwards he claimed he

could resurrect the dead, which gave some of his
followers reservations about his credibility. When one
of his members died of cancer later that year he stood
vigil over his decomposing body for two months,
chanting 'Rise! Rise!' with increasing desperation.
The police eventually got wind of his escapade and
raided the premises, charging him with failure to
report the death. Ten years later he jumped to his
death from his tenth floor apartment, which may or
may not have been suicide. As well as resurrecting the
dead, the latterday messiah also fancied he would be
able to fly if put to it.

Marjorie Gortner

This Hollywood actress was a former child evangelist
who performed her first marriage ceremony at the age
of four in 1949.

Thomas Offitz

Construction worker in Norfolk, Virginia, who saw a
strange brand on his hand one day in the 1980s. He
interpreted it as the '666' mark of the devil and
proceeded to slice it off at the wrist with his chainsaw.
His co-workers were horrified at his action and had
the hand frozen in ice and Thomas airlifted to the
nearest hospital where doctors told him they could
re-attach it. Thomas declined the offer, but some
months later he sued the doctors for abiding by his
silly wish. He was looking for $144,000
compensation, but left the court empty-handed.

RESOURCEFUL-NESS

Captain James Cook (1728-79)

This acclaimed navigator and cartographer devised a subtle use of reverse psychology during a sailing expedition when he feared an outbreak of scurvy among his crew. He believed the German dish of sauerkraut would prevent this but also knew his sailors hated it. To get them to eat it he put a huge sign on his ship over his supply: 'For Use Of The Captain And Officers Only.' It disappeared before long, and the disease was indeed averted.

Jemmy Hirst (1738-1829)

Opportunist farmer from Rawcliffe who kept a coffin in his kitchen and served drinks to his guests from it. This was no ordinary coffin, mind, for it had windows on it and shelves inside. He stood it up vertically and asked visitors to his house to stand in it to see if they liked it. As soon as they did so, the door locked on them. Jemmy charged them a penny to open it and let them out.

Francis Henry Egerton (1756-1829)

The 8th Earl of Bridgewater had a penchant for shooting birds. When his eyesight failed he came up with a novel method of continuing the sport. He enabled himself to continue his hobby by bringing the mountain to Mohammad, as it were. He asked his servants to clip the wings off a number of pigeons and partridges. He could then take potshots at them as they scuttled round his grounds without the escape hatch of flight available.

Sir Francis Galton (1822-1911)

This 19th-century scientist came up with a simple way of keeping one's clothes dry during a rainstorm: take them off and sit on them.

Irvin S. Cobb (1876-1944)

When the American humorist was out of a job at the age of 30 with a wife and sick child to support, he became rather desperate when every effort to get work with newspapers fell flat. He finally decided to pen a round robin letter to a selection of them, adopting an aggressive pose to hide his desperation. The letter went: 'This is positively your last chance. I have grown weary of studying the wallpaper designs in your ante-room. A modest appreciation of my worth forbids my doing business with your head office boy any longer. Unless you grab me right away, I will go elsewhere and leave your paper flat on its back right here in the middle of a hard summer, and your whole life hereafter will be one vast, surging regret.' Somehow or other the letter hit a chord and the next day Irvin got four job offers.

Clara Bow (1905-65)

The actress put soil all over the floor of one of the rooms in her house so her dog could go to the toilet on it rather than have to go outdoors.

Bill Ridding

Trainer of Bolton Wanderers soccer team in the late 1940s who discovered that his team's shinguards were missing as they arrived at a venue for a match. Ridding solved the situation by buying 22 slim paperback novels and using them instead.

Colonel Tom Parker

Elvis Presley's opportunistic manager had a previous career as a carnival huckster. One of his moneymaking pursuits was charging people to see chickens 'dancing' on a hot griddle.

ROMANTIC NONSENSE

Karl Wilhelm von Humboldt (1767-1835)

The German statesman and linguist composed a one hundred line poem in honour of his wife on 40 consecutive days.

Lady Caroline Lamb (1785-1828)

During her passionate affair with Lord Byron, she sent him a tuft of her pubic hair as a sign of devotion. She asked for one back in return, but not before telling him to be careful with the scissors.

George Osbaldeston (1786-1866)

This gentleman was known as 'The Squire of All England' due to his fine horsemanship. He once rode 25 miles to find a rare orchid to impress a woman.

Gabriel D'Annunzio (1883-1938)

During his affair with the actress Eleanora Duse his passion reached new heights. They doted on one another so much, in fact, that one year for his birthday she sent him a telegram attesting to her love every hour for 12 hours. When she died he professed to be able to communicate with her spirit by chewing a pomegranate while praying before a statue of Buddha.

Benito Mussolini (1883-1945)

Eloped with Rachele Guidi, one of the pupils at the school where his mother taught, in 1915. When her parents objected, he pulled out a pistol and said to them. 'Here are six bullets: one for Rachele, five for me'. They then relented and accepted the couple.

Salvador Dali (1904-89)

The eccentric surrealist artist tried to make himself attractive to Gala, the woman of his dreams, by shaving his armpits until they bled and wearing his own peculiar brand of perfume made from fish glue and cow dung.

Tom Jones (1940-)

After he became famous the singer shipped his local telephone kiosk from Pontypridd in Wales to his Bel Air home in California because he had once used it to phone his sweetheart, Linda, who subsequently became his wife.

Hal Jarrold

A Texan farmer bought a jet in 1970 for an unusual reason: it was the plane in which, eight years before, he had tried to get off with a lady but failed. In an attempt to recapture something of her spirit, he dismantled the plane and re-built it as a summer house for his garden.

ROYAL NUTTERS

Mithridrates (?-63BC)

This ancient king, fearing he was going to be poisoned by his subjects, ingested small amounts of poison daily in the hope of rendering himself immune to its effects. His ploy worked, but when he was defeated by the Romans he tried to kill himself by taking it and it didn't work. Outdone by his own cleverness, he was forced to order one of his soldiers to stab him.

Ethelred (968-1016)

English king who was beaten so severely with candles by his mother as a child that for the rest of his life he refused to have them carried in front of him in processions.

Kubla Khan (1215-94)

The Mongol emperor ordered his servants to stuff silk napkins into their mouths when in his presence as it would have been unthinkable for him to breathe the same air as they did.

Henry VIII (1491-1547)

Was so fanatical about poisoning the memory of Thomas à Becket that, 350 years after his death, he had his corpse dug up and his skeleton tried and convicted of treason, and subsequently burned.

Queen Elizabeth I (1533-1603)

Elizabeth may have had the body of a feeble woman, but apparently she had the tongue of the most foul-mouthed man and would swear savagely when angry. She once spat at a courtier because she didn't like his clothing. Elizabeth was also prone to fits of hysteria and, when she thought none of her courtiers were looking, would throw up her arms laughing and skip around the garden.

Charles II (1661-1700)

Two of his servants always accompanied this Spanish king to the toilet: one to hold a candle and the other the toilet paper.

Peter the Great (1672-1725)

The Russian Tsar played with toy soldiers on his bed on his wedding night as his bewildered wife Catherine wondered what she had married. He consummated his marriage with her ten years later, but by then (perhaps understandably) she had found herself another lover. When Peter found out about this he decapitated the man and had the head pickled in a jar which he put on her bedside locker to warn her against any further indiscretions.

At one period of his life Peter formed the notion that he wanted to be a dentist, which resulted in him extracting teeth from virtually anyone he met.

Philip V (1683-1746)

Eighteenth-century Spanish king who first began to show signs of derangement in 1717 when he became consumed by what he called an 'internal fire' – the sun striking his shoulder and sending piercing rays into the centre of his body. He felt he was about to die but his doctors could find nothing at all amiss. This caused him great melancholia, eventually resulting in him abdicating the throne. Towards the end of his life he somehow formed the notion that his feet were different sizes, which made him give up walking altogether.

Queen Victoria (1819-1901)

Disgruntled by a rough crossing to Ireland, she sent a note up to the captain of the ship saying: 'Don't let this happen again!'

Princess Alexandra

This 19th-century Bavarian princess, sister of King Maximilian II and aunt of 'Mad King' Ludwig II, believed she had swallowed a glass grand piano as a child.

Ludwig II (1845-86)

Madcap Bavarian king who heard voices from the age of 14 and was prone to some rather unusual habits, like getting up in the middle of the night to ride round his palace in a horse-drawn sleigh decorated with cherubs. In 1865 he installed an artificial moon and stars on the ceiling of his bedroom to give himself the illusion that he was sleeping outside. He also talked to plants and trees with great passion.

Ludwig was so shy he needed up to ten glasses of champagne for social occasions. At these he ordered huge bouquets of flowers to be placed in front of his throne so that he couldn't be seen by the guests. He liked the music to be played at mega-decibel levels so that he wouldn't have to talk to such guests in the unfortunate circumstance of him being spotted. He dined frequently with one of his mares, who usually rode roughshod over the plates and cutlery after he had eaten, thus obviating the inconvenience of anyone having to wash up.

Abdul Aziz

Nineteenth-century sultan of the Ottoman Empire who had 5000 servants, not all of whom worked all hours. One of them had nothing to do but reset the counters on Abdul's backgammon board between games. Another was employed to keep an eye on his fingernails and snip them at intervals.

King Farouk (1920-65)

Though filthy rich, the last King of Egypt's favourite hobby was picking people's pockets at parties, often netting himself a tidy haul of jewellery from his well-heeled guests.

He was also particularly fond of pop and drank over 30 bottles of fizzy orange drinks every day.

SADISTS

Tiberius (42BC-AD37)

The Roman emperor was a cruel despot, achieving great pleasure from getting people drunk and then knotting a cord so tightly round their genitals that it cut into their flesh and prevented them from relieving themselves of all the wine he poured down their gullets.

Nero (AD37-68)

Kicked his wife to death when she revealed that he was late home for dinner. Consumed with guilt afterwards, he saw a man who resembled her in appearance and married him – after first having him castrated. Nero's favourite party game involved him wearing the skin of a wild animal and being let loose from a cage into a room where men and women were tied to stakes. He would then savage their private parts.

Ivan the Terrible (1536-84)

This incorrigible Russian Tsar was forever devising new methods of torture to entertain himself. He had one of his victims roasted alive, and had another sewn into a bearskin and hunted down by a pack of hounds. He had dogs thrown off towers, cats roasted alive and thousands of people executed, including his own son.

He once nailed a man's hat to his head, and another's foot to the floor, but spent his last years as a repentant monk.

Louis XIV (1638-1715)

The French king ordered the noses and ears of prostitutes consorting with his soldiers to be cut off in 1674.

Anna Ivanovna (1693-1740)

Unpredictable Russian Empress who once punished three of her courtiers by ordering them to live as hens for a week. They had to wear costumes bedecked with feathers and sit on eggs in baskets stuffed with straw, and cluck repeatedly in front of large audiences before she forgave them for what was only a paltry offence in the first place.

Erzebet Bathory

Seventeenth-century Hungarian noblewoman who tortured over 600 young girls, having locked them up in cages and spiked them to death at her leisure.

Marquis de Sade (1740-1814)

The man from whom the word 'sadism' comes rationalised his beatings, sodomy, flagellation, blasphemy etc. by a messianic belief in himself. 'It always seemed to me,' he said once, 'that everything must give in to me, that the whole world must flatter my whims, and that it was up to me alone to conceive and satisfy them.' He once whipped a girl with a knotted rope when she was naked, then poured hot wax into her wounds.

Joan Crawford (1906-77)

The actress made 'night raids' on her children, waking them up in the middle of the night to complain about some minor household task that wasn't executed to her wishes, and throttling them with wire hangers as punishment. She pulled lumps out of their hair and made them re-polish floors until they could almost see their reflections in them.

Bette Davis (1908-89)

Wore heavy weights strapped to her body in a scene from *Whatever Happened to Baby Jane* in which her co-star Joan Crawford had to lift her. The pair of them were engaged in a feud that lasted decades.

SEX

George II (1683-1760)

Had sex with his mistress at precisely nine o'clock every night, growing deeply distressed if he missed his deadline by even a minute.

Giovanni Casanova (1725-98)

Made love to 132 women in his life, a tally that isn't huge considering his reputation in this regard. That number comprised servants, members of the royalty, prostitutes, nuns and even a theologian. He had sex with one woman 12 times in one 24 hour period. For contraception he sometimes constructed a dia-phragm from a lemon. Casanova was also a proponent of incest, remarking once, 'I have never been able to understand how a father could tenderly love his charming daughter without having slept with her at least once.'

Catherine the Great (1729-96)

The Russian empress was alleged to have had sex six times a day claiming it was to cure her insomnia. She was even supposed to have copulated with a horse on one occasion.

Victor Hugo (1802-85)

A womaniser throughout his life, Hugo made love to his wife nine times on his wedding night. He had an affair with a 27-year-old laundress when he was 70. Thirteen years later he was still sexually active.

Hans Christian Andersen (1805-75)

The writer of fairytales visited brothels, but for no other motive than to speak to the prostitutes.

Frank Harris (1854-1931)

This author kept a record of all his lovers – reputed to number over 2000 – and deposited the details with Lloyd's of London for safe keeping, insuring the file in question for $150,000. His book, *My Life and Loves*, based on this list, was banned for 40 years in the U.S. and U.K. but it sold well in Parisian bookshops.

George Bernard Shaw (1856-1950)

The playwright and essayist was so upset by losing his virginity to an elderly widow at the age of 29 that he didn't attempt sexual relations with another woman for 15 years afterwards.

Gabriele D'Annunzio (1863-1938)

This Italian author and aviator had such an active libido he even carried condoms into battle with him, because a man had to be prepared for every eventuality. He's also said to have used strychnine as an aphrodisiac.

Marie Stopes (1880-1958)

A lifelong advocate of free sex, Stopes established the first birth control clinic in Great Britain. Though she was passionate about the right of women to enjoy the pleasures of the flesh without the baggage of puritanical guilt – a luxury that a repressed past had denied them, in her view – she had precious little knowledge of the subject herself. Her female friends enlightened her as to what an orgasm was when she was 36, and the news came as something of a shock to her. Shortly afterwards she was divorced from her husband. A lawyer at her divorce case in 1916 had the temerity to ask her if he had ever had an erection, and she replied enigmatically, 'I remember three occasions when he was partially rigid, but never effectively so'.

Two years later Marie re-married and this time she did indeed lose her virginity: to fellow birth control campaigner Humphrey Roe. Like many late developers, she was demanding in bed and Humphrey wasn't able to satisfy her much more than her former husband. After they had been married 20 years she made him write a letter testifying to his deficiencies, which in effect gave her *carte blanche* to be unfaithful to him. It was an opportunity she wasn't shy to grasp, though she was nearly 60 at the time.

Recent studies of Stopes's life have suggested that she had a dual purpose in campaigning for birth control. As well as the sexual licence it afforded, they contend, she was also something of an ethnic cleanser and campaigned for the enforced sterility of those she deemed racially inferior.

D.H. Lawrence (1885-1930)

Was turned off by any woman who got pleasure from sex, seeing this as a strictly male preserve.

Babe Ruth (1895-1948)

The American baseball player had such a voracious sexual appetite he once took over a whole brothel for the night, making love to every prostitute in it and celebrating his performance the next morning with an omelette made of 18 eggs.

Georges Simenon (1903-89)

Made love to over 10,000 women in his life. He often used to have sex with four different women in a day. Neither did he draw the line at prostitutes, wives of his friends, or servants. (One of the duties of his house-maid Boule was to wake him after his lunchtime siesta so they could make love.) When asked why he was so licentious, he replied, 'It wasn't in any way a vice. I simply needed to communicate. The only way to really get to know a woman is to have sex with her.'

Elvis Presley (1935-77)

Installed two-way mirrors in Graceland to watch his bodyguards make out with their girlfriends and wives. The singer hated the idea of having sex with any women who had given birth, including Priscilla, his wife.

Ted Gainor

This unfortunate gentleman suffered whiplash at a strip club one night in 1983 in Florida when a feisty damsel buried her breasts in his face, causing his head to jerk backwards. He described them as being like 'two cement blocks' and sued for damages. The said mammaries were weighed in court but adjudged to be of 'average firmness' by the judge, who dismissed the claim.

SKINFLINTS

Sarah Jennings (1660-1744)

The First Duchess of Marlborough and influential member of the Whig party economised on ink by not dotting her i's or using full stops.

Daniel Dancer (1716-94)

Daniel inherited a great deal of property from his Middlesex father, but you'd never think it from the way he lived. Existing on famine-style rations in the house he shared with his sister, he even refused to call a doctor when she became dangerously ill, telling people that whatever happened would be the will of God. After she died he continued his stingy ways, wearing clothes until they almost fell off him and importuning strangers for money and food in subtle ways, which gave him enormous satisfaction.

He came across the rotting carcass of a sheep one day while out walking and brought it home and skinned it, having the decaying meat made into pies and feeding the bones to his dog. He obtained fertiliser for his fields by stuffing his pocket with cow dung. When he received a gift of a fish that had been frozen during transport, he was too mean to heat it over a fire, deciding to sit on it instead until it had thawed out. As he found soap and towels too expensive, Daniel waited for sunny days to wash himself. He went to a pond and lay in the sun afterwards until he was dry.

His favourite hobby was counting his many thousands of pounds like Silas Marner. After he died, wads of notes were found in jugs, cabinets and containers – and even up the chimney.

Thomas Cooke (1726-1811)

This American sugar magnate (not to be confused with Thomas Cook, the travel pioneer) was worth over £100,000 when he died. Despite this, however, he was known to fall in people's doors pretending to be ill so they would give him free glasses of wine to revive him. He was religiously inclined, but preferred to receive Holy Communion at home to avoid having to put a shilling in the church plate. When he was dying, he threw his doctor out of the house for prescribing costly medicine for him to ease his pain.

John Elwes (1730-89)

A nephew of the fabulously rich Sir Harvey Elwes, John twigged early in life that he would be the chief beneficiary of Sir Harvey's legacy and did his best to please him in his last years. Sir Harvey was famous for his parsimony, so they passed their evenings sitting round a grim fire until bedtime. Elwes inherited £250,000 when Sir Harvey finally died in 1763. Instead of spending the money, he made it his life's work to add to it, living the life of a pauper as he accumulated properties all over London.

Whenever he was travelling he brought a hard-boiled egg in his pocket with him so that he wouldn't have to stop somewhere to eat. He took back roads to avoid toll charges and rode his horse on grass to avoid wear and tear on its shoes. At home he went to bed as soon as it got dark to save money on candles. He refused to light a fire even when soaking wet from

SKINFLINTS

walking in the rain. He dressed himself from beggars'
cast-offs found in ditches. He slept on bare boards
because he deemed sheets and blankets to be too
much of an extravagance.

He hated paying doctors but once he bruised his
legs badly and was forced to have one summoned.
Even then, however, his opportunistic brain went into
overdrive. After the doctor had told him he needed
treatment, he begged to disagree. He made a bet with
the man, allowing him to apply his remedy to one of
the legs and to leave the other alone. If the untreated
one healed as quickly as the treated one, he asked to
be excused of the fee. And of course he was right.
Another guinea saved for posterity! This exemplar of
frugality left more than £750,000 in his will.

John Camden Neild (1780-1852)

Nineteenth-century businessman who inherited
£250,000 but dressed like a tramp and went about the
streets seeking alms and hitching lifts from passing
carriages to save himself money on public transport.
When he died he left all his money to Queen Victoria,
ignoring family and friends, and even a woman who
had saved his life when he attempted suicide in 1828.

Morgan Jones (1781-1824)

Miserly Welsh vicar who arrived in the parish of
Blewbury in 1798 and wore the same coat from that
day until his death 26 years later. When the lining got
tattered he simply turned it inside out, thereafter

cutting off the tails and using them as patches. When the brim of his hat wore away he took a replacement from a scarecrow.

Langton Freeman

Eighteenth-century Warwickshire rector who was so tightfisted that when he lodged with parishioners he removed threads from their blankets to mend his clothes.

Hetty Green (1836-1916)

One of the most reviled women in America in her time, Hetty was a Massachusetts lady who inherited $4 million at the age of 30 when her father died, but lived like a pauper afterwards, dressing herself in shabby clothes and mismatched stockings, living in cheap boarding-houses and travelling round New York in a carriage that had once been used as a hen house. She was even too stingy to procure an office for herself, conducting her business at a desk given to her in her local bank, surrounded by trunks and documents and looking for all the world like a demented bag lady. One might imagine they would have been glad of her business, but her poor hygiene turned other customers away, and the fact that she wanted to have all her money available to her for use meant the bank couldn't use it.

She later inherited another $1 million from an aunt, and decided to marry so that her money wouldn't pass to the aunt's next of kin after she died. She betrothed herself to Ed Green in 1867. They separated afterwards but he had performed the function she wanted in giving her two children, Ned and Sylvia. Ed died in 1902 and Hetty wore widow's weeds for the rest of her life – not so much from grief but because black required less maintenance than any other colour!

She heated oatmeal on a radiator to feed her children. After she read the morning paper she would send Ned back out onto the street to re-sell it. If he didn't succeed, she would tell him to stuff it inside his jumper to keep warm instead of having to shell out on an extra vest. One day Ned dislocated his kneecap and she was too mean to call the doctor and tried to heal it herself. When she failed, she took him down to the local hospital in disguise, trying to pass him off as a charity case. When she was recognised, she beat a hasty retreat. As a result, the leg became gangrenous and had to be amputated.

She suffered a stroke in 1916. Ned employed nurses to look after her but warned them to dress in their streetclothes or they would be dismissed as Hetty was all too well aware of the cost of professional home help. She died shortly afterwards, but few of those who attended her funeral in New Bedford shed tears over her passing. A biography of her was entitled *The Witch of Wall Street*.

Sir George Reresby Sitwell (1860-1943)

The father of Osbert and Edith, this dotty gentleman was seriously rich but refused to install electricity in his Derbyshire mansion, working with candles in all the rooms instead to save money. Penny-wise and pound-foolish, he went on to employ 4000 labourers to make a lake in his grounds. Sitwell was noted for quibbling over trivial bills and then splashing out thousands of pounds on works of art. He hated entertaining because of the expense involved, and rationalised it away by saying, 'To be financially safe, one should be friendless'.

James Eads How (1868-1930)

How inherited $250,000 when his mother died but had a conscience about accepting unearned cash so put it under the mattress and took to the roads like a hobo, foraging for work wherever he could and dressing like a tramp. So ragged was his appearance, he was often arrested for vagrancy. He fell into bad health due to hardship and a poor diet, holding the belief that any bodily ailment could be cured by total abstinence from food.

As he neared death in Cincinnati in 1930 he made out a will leaving only $5 each to a brother and stepson, and the minimum entitled by law to his ex-wife. This wasn't from meanness, but an exercise of the same frugality by which he lived his own life. The remainder of his estate he donated to charity and the education of the unemployed. This had ironically quadrupled since he inherited it since he hadn't invested it and thus it hadn't depreciated during the Depression.

J. Paul Getty (1892-1976)

The multi-millionaire oil magnate and art collector was notoriously mean. When his grandson was kidnapped, he refused to pay the ransom until the boy's ear was mailed to him. When he got a present of a watch from a German friend he refused it because he was informed he would have had to pay import duty on it.

He had phone boxes installed in one of his mansions to prevent guests cadging free calls from him. The reason he gave for the installation of the phones was to save his guests the embarrassment of having to 'settle up' with him. He answered begging letters apologetically but firmly, claiming that his wealth was overstated and that the government took a lot of it in taxes. And besides, he wasn't in the business of charity.

John Christie (1882-1962)

This wealthy founder of the Glyndebourne Festival Opera refused to tip waiters, explaining to them (conveniently) that he felt it would be patronising to them to do so. A *bon viveur* who threw lavish parties, he spent hundreds of pounds on champagne, but steamed unused stamps off letters to re-use them and refused to light fires even on freezing cold nights, preferring to carry a small electric fire with him from room to room, plugging it in to a socket near where he decided to sit. Christie often turned out the lights in a room where people were chatting, leaving them to continue their talks in the darkness. He worried so much about his electricity bill he eventually employed a man to do nothing more than ensure all the lights in his house were turned off when they should be.

Nizam of Hyderabad (1884-1967)

This Indian Prince donated £25 million to the British Exchequer to help with expenses incurred during the First World War. Such largesse was followed by bouts of frugality, the nadir being reached when he allowed guests at his palace only one cigarette each – and then smoked the butts they left in their ash-trays himself after they had departed. He also insisted on punctuality and fined guests who were late for his *soirées*.

It is told that he once invited an expert in pearls to come out from England to value his collection. So vast was it that the man told the Nizam the task would take two years. "I can't afford that," said the Nizam and sent him back to England.

Vita Sackville-West (1892-1962)

Although wealthy, the writer and garden designer was so parsimonious that she avoided spending money on paper by writing letters to people on envelopes, the edges of newspapers and, on one occasion at least, on an old piece of ham. To avoid having to buy stamps she used unused ones from old letters.

Ernest Onians (1895-1985)

Antiques collector from Suffolk who was spectacularly rich but never bought his wife a present in 40 years of marriage. Onians once dismissed a cleaning lady for vacuuming a carpet too well, and thus being deemed guilty of wearing out its threads.

Gary Cooper (1901-61)

Liked paying for products by cheque because he knew his celebrity status was such, the cheques would more likely be framed than cashed.

Cary Grant (1904-86)

Even after he became a millionaire, Grant used to save the strings off parcels for re-use. He also recycled unsuitable gifts at Christmas to avoid having to fork out cash for his own ones.

Aristotle Onassis (1906-75)

Onassis was so rich he owned his own bank, but was noted for quibbling about a few dollars on bills. He refused to wear an overcoat because he would have had to buy an expensive one, then insured it, and then tip the hat check people everywhere he went. He saved about $20,000 a year braving the elements.

SLEEP

William Wilkie (1721-72)

The sleeping conditions of this Scottish poet beggared belief. He hated clean sheets, and when he was staying at someone's house he had to inform his host that he would make his own bedding arrangements. He invariably brought his own dirty sheets with him ... and two dozen blankets to go on top of them.

Benjamin Disraeli (1804-81)

The British Prime Minister and novelist used to sleep in a bed with its four legs immersed in bowls of salt to ward off evil spirits.

William Ewart Gladstone (1809-98)

Used to take a stone hot water bottle to bed with him, filling it with tea. He only slept for a few hours a night and used to drink the tea when he awoke as it was still lukewarm.

Charles Dickens (1812-70)

Couldn't sleep or write, unless he was facing north. To ward off insomnia he always lay in the centre of his bed, measuring the distance to both edges with his arms to make sure they were exactly the same.

S LEEP

Alexander Graham Bell (1847-1922)

The inventor had to stay up all night anytime he had an early morning appointment as he suffered from ferocious headaches upon waking every day.

Dwight Eisenhower (1890-1969)

The U.S. general and president kept a shotgun beside his bed to shoot crows, cats and anything else that disturbed his sleep.

James Thurber (1894-1961)

A chronic insomniac, Thurber tried everything in the book to get to sleep, including spelling words backwards and rewriting Edgar Allen Poe's *The Raven* from the viewpoint of the bird.

Clara Bow (1905-65)

The first 'It' Girl was a lifelong insomniac after a childhood experience of her mother charging into her bedroom one night armed with a butcher's knife trying to stab her.

Joan Didion (1934-)

The Californian writer slept in the same room as her manuscripts when she was composing them, viewing them as children she wanted to be near.

SPORT

Lord Frederick Beauclerk (1773-1850)

This Hertfordshire vicar seemed to be more fascinated by cricket than religion. Neither was he averse to rigging matches, or boasting about the fact afterwards. Beauclerk often pretended to be injured or disabled to 'throw' the opposition. He also rode horses at Epsom under assumed names so that his bishop wouldn't find out about it. The seat in his pulpit was – fittingly – in the shape of a saddle.

Jamie Duff

Eighteenth-century racing buff from Edinburgh who was perusing the rules of the turf one day when he noticed that they didn't specify a horse had to have four legs and a tail. Jamie seized his opportunity and entered himself, running the race on foot, though in the pose of a jockey, with his knees bent and his bottom stuck out. Sadly, he didn't prove to be as fast as the steeds he raced against, despite whipping himself repeatedly in the thigh to goad himself on.

David Harris

This Hambledon cricketer from the late 18th century, one of the great bowlers of the early years of cricket, refused to retire even when assailed by gout in his later years, making his way to bowl on crutches and insisting on being allowed to rest in his wicker armchair between deliveries.

Queen Alexandra (1844-1925)

This Danish monarch – the wife of Edward VII – somehow imagined that golf was governed by the same rules as hockey, and that the idea was to prevent one's opponent putting the ball into the hole. This led to many scrimmages on greens. She also thought that the person who got the ball into the hole first won the game, so she constantly pressurised her colleagues to speed up as they studied their shots.

Rudyard Kipling (1865-1936)

The author was so fond of golf he painted his golf balls red one day so he could play in the snow.

Walter Breeze Smith

President of the Tuxedo Golf Club in New York in the early 1900s, Smith had a glass eye which he enjoyed taking out to show people at every available opportunity. Giving a whole new meaning to the term 'keeping your eye on the ball', during one match he brought 18 substitute eyes with him and placed one on his ball at every tee, smashing it to smithereens every time he took a shot. After he won the match he took his victory as proof of the veracity of the above maxim.

Gaston Vareilles

French international rugby player who lacked something in the way of commitment to the game. On a train journey to a venue in 1911 (Scotland was the adversary) he stopped off at a junction to buy a sandwich because he was feeling peckish. The train left the station without him and he missed the game. That was effectively the end of his career. It was an expensive sandwich.

Shinzo Kanaguri

Japanese athlete who dropped out of the 1912 Olympic marathon in Stockholm because he saw a family having a picnic on the side of the road and decided on a whim to join them. He informed none of the authorities of his decision so was officially declared a missing person until he returned to Japan the following day.

Albert Camus (1913-60)

As well as being a writer, Camus was also goalkeeper for a local Algerian side, even going so far as to testify that he learned more about morality from this activity than he did from all of his reading.

Bill Werbeniuk (1947-)

Canadian snooker player noted for his weight, which fluctuates round the 20 stone mark, largely due to the fact that his doctors recommend he drinks up to 25 pints of lager a day to alleviate a condition called 'familial benign essential tremor'. It's a nervous disorder that makes his arms shake and the only known cure is ingesting vast amounts of lager. His friend and colleague Cliff Thorburn says that a drug appeared on the market some years ago that could substitute for the liquor but Bill refused to consider it for fear of becoming an addict.

During the early 1980s, the best spell of Werbeniuk's career (at one point he was ranked eighth in the world), he lived in England in a converted bus which doubled as a mobile home to save himself the expense of hotel bills going from venue to venue. It was kitted out with all the mod cons – including draught lager!

Bill Veeck

Manager of a St. Louis baseball team in the 1950s who, after a string of humiliating defeats, decided desperate situations required desperate remedies so he started offering gifts to the public to watch his shambolic team perform. These included orchids flown in from Hawaii, cakes, live lobsters, baseball bats (he bought 6000 of these from a manufacturer who was going out of business and remaindering them) and even stepladders. Another draw for the crowd was a scoreboard from which fireworks would erupt on the (very) odd occasion that the team scored. It also played Handel's 'Messiah' to celebrate such rarities.

Veeck's most original ploy was to sell miniature hot dogs during time-outs and have them distributed by midgets. This worked so well he even put one of the midgets on his team, but sadly he performed just as badly as the rest of the players. Although the fans returned to the game for a while, the team's abysmal run continued unabated and eventually the team was dumped from the league.

Gary Winram

This Australian swimmer was so anxious to win the National Championships in 1956 that before they got under way he had himself hypnotised to believe he was being chased by a shark. Alas, it didn't work and he only came second.

Pedro Wingie

A Texan who walked around the world backwards in 1960 carrying a sandwich board that transmitted his intentions to those he passed in a variety of languages. He traversed Asia, Europe and the U.S., usually clocking up about 45 miles a day, a rear-view mirror attached to his glasses to ensure he didn't bump into things in his perambulations. His motive? To win a £200 bet he placed with a friend to prove he could do it. When he had completed the task, he found he much

preferred walking backwards to forwards and
continued to do so for the rest of his life.

Kenneth Baily

This Bournemouth civil servant decided in the mid-
1960s that he would become Britain's sporting mascot
so duly kitted himself out in a top hat, hunting coat,
Union Jack waistcoat and national flag.

Since then he's travelled all over the world as
the country's self-appointed standard-bearer. So
ostentatious is Baily's get-up that when Prince
Charles met him he said, 'Where did you escape
from?'

Charlie Sheen (1965-)

The actor once bought all 2,615 seats behind the left-
field fence at a baseball stadium in the hope of catching
a home-run ball.

Minna Wilson

Mother of light heavyweight boxer Steve McCarthy
who was getting a bit of a hammering from his
opponent in a bout in Southampton in 1989. Rallying
to her son's cause, she leaped into the ring and started
battering the man with her high heels. She cut him so
badly he couldn't go on with the fight and was
disqualified. But a re-match was subsequently
arranged and she was banned from the ringside.

SUPERSTITIONS

Prince Urusoff

Russian nobleman who was on his honeymoon on the Black Sea when his new bride dropped her wedding ring into the water by accident. According to an old family superstition, this presaged her death so he decided to 'buy' the sea (at a cost of $40 million) in the belief that if he owned it, he still owned the ring sitting at the bottom. The good news is that his wife didn't die until she was a very old lady, but after she did, Urusoff's children sold the sea again – for twice the price.

Charles Stewart Parnell (1846-91)

This Irish statesman was so superstitious, whenever he found himself walking from his driveway to his house he felt it was bad luck if the number of footsteps he took ended in multiples of four. If they did, he walked back to the driveway and tried again, taking longer or shorter strides.

Enrico Caruso (1873-1921)

The Italian operatic tenor refused to wear a new suit on a Friday. Whenever he donned a new one on any other day, he put a good luck coin into one of the pockets.

James Joyce (1882-1941)

A man of many superstitions, Joyce made it a habit to carry objects like rings and rabbits' ears with him to ward off evil powers. He was also superstitious about empty bottles on tables bringing bad luck and always removed them when he saw them.

John Wayne (1907-79)

If he was playing poker and a card turned face up by accident, he made the person to whom it had been dealt stand up and circle the table three times.

Joe DiMaggio (1914-)

This legendary baseball player began a winning streak of hits the day after he dated a Broadway chorus girl. He dated her until the streak ran out, imagining it was she who was responsible for them.

Zsa Zsa Gabor (1919-)

Believes that if a mirror breaks, you have to go to Paris, stand on the Pont Alexandre III and throw the pieces over your shoulder into the Seine or you'll have bad luck all your life.

Gillo Pontecorvo (1919-)

This temperamental director always wore the same overcoat for the first shot of a movie. He didn't allow the colour purple on his sets, and wouldn't answer questions put to him on Thursdays. If somebody spilled salt in his presence, he ran round a table throwing more salt in all directions to keep demons at bay. If wine was spilt, he made the guilty party dip his or her finger in it and daub it behind the ear of everyone present.

Truman Capote (1924-84)

The writer had a variety of superstitions and refused to telephone people whose phone numbers added up to an 'unlucky figure'. He wouldn't accept certain hotel rooms for the same reason. Capote wouldn't sit at a table where there were three cigarette butts in an ashtray, or travel on a plane that had two nuns on it, and refused to begin or end anything on a Friday.

Luciano Pavarotti (1935-)

The Italian tenor won't sing unless he finds a bent nail on the stage floor of the auditorium in which he's appearing. The metal is for good luck and it has to be bent to simulate horns that ward off evil. Fans from all over the world have sent him bent nails in the post since they heard him saying this, but they're no good to him as he has to find one on the actual floor of the venue where he's appearing.

Barry Manilow (1946-)

Has a clause in his contract stating that nobody may cross his path from the time he leaves his dressing room to when he steps onto the stage.

Bjorn Borg (1956-)

His famous designer stubble resulted from a superstition that he wouldn't win Wimbledon if he shaved before it started; it proved lucky for him for five consecutive years before John McEnroe dethroned him in 1981.

Another device he used to keep on the right side of Lady Luck was to ensure that the car driving him to the venue had a radio. If matches went to a final set, he asked his mother to suck a sweet during crucial moments, which she always did.

Goran Ivanisevic (1971-)

Like Borg, he doesn't shave or cut his hair once a tennis tournament has begun, and on match days gets up at exactly the same time. He refuses to use the same shower or toilet on successive days even if it means ignoring an empty cubicle and queueing up. It paid off at Wimbledon in 2001.

Alexander Wurz (1974-)

Austrian racing driver and Formula 1 star, Wurz wears a red boot on his left foot and a blue one on his right. He won his first major race in New Zealand the day he did this by accident (a prankster had hidden the ones he was intending to wear so he had to put on the first ones he saw because of time pressure) so he's continued the practice.

TALENTS

Peter Beales

Acclaimed Elizabethan calligrapher who lettered the entire Bible in a walnut shell no bigger than a hen's egg.

Sam Bisset

Born in Perth in 1721, Bisset had some rather unusual talents. He taught monkeys to dance on tightropes, cats to play tunes on dulcimers, canaries to spell, rabbits to beat drums with their hind-legs and turtles to fetch and carry like dogs.

On a trip to Dublin in 1782, Bisset attempted to train a black suckling pig he bought at a market. Sixteen months later the porcine prodigy was able to spell out names, solve mathematical problems, tell the time and even point out words on flashcards that were suggested by the audiences before which he performed. After one show, however, an official expressed disdain about the manner in which Bisset earned his living, and threatened the life of the pig.

Bisset became so agitated as a result of the abuse that he died shortly afterwards en route to Chester with his pet.

Ivan Ivanitz Chabert (1792-?)

Born in France, Chabert was known as 'The Human Salamander' because of his ability to enter a blazing oven with two raw steaks in his hands and emerge some minutes later looking just as he entered... but with the steaks cooked to perfection. He was also able to put boiling lead into his mouth, inhale the vapours of arsenic dipped in fire, rub a red hot shovel on his tongue, arms and legs, and eat burning charcoal. As an encore to his act, he offered to undergo torture by fire as practised in the Spanish Inquisition.

He once even swallowed an ounce of arsenic, 30 grams of phosphorus and a large quantity of nitric acid. After being challenged to swallow a teaspoonful of prussic acid he did so, but not before ingesting his own special antidote. When asked to reveal the nature of this antidote for the great benefits it could have for medical research, he demanded 10,000 guineas for the revelation. Nobody was prepared to pay and he was dismissed as a trickster.

Daniel Wildman

Eighteenth-century English aviarist and horseman who had a truly unique talent. Standing on top of a horse with a swarm of bees buzzing round his head,

he was able to command them to return to their hive
by firing a pistol. He sometimes controlled up to three
separate swarms simultaneously. His technique
involved tying a fine thread round the thorax of the
queen bee, tugging it gently to achieve the
movements he wanted. Once he had the queen in tow,
the rest followed her lead.

Alvin Kelly (1885-1952)

American stuntman who specialised in steeplejack
capers. After his movie career ended he took to doing
handstands on flagpoles perched on the top of high
rises in Dallas, Texas. By 1928 he was making $100 a
day for his antics, a phenomenal price for the
Depression era. He was able to stay motionless for
hours on the spin, relieving nature by means of a
secret hose he hooked up to the flagpole. Sometimes
he sat on a chair attached to the pole, even managing
to doze off sometimes by locking his thumbs into the
shaft so that he couldn't fall off. In 1939 he was hired
to promote National Doughnut Week by standing on
his head on a plank perched on a skyscraper 54 floors
above ground level in New York, eating 13
doughnuts.

Thea Alba

Born in Berlin in the early 1900s, Alba demonstrated
some unique skills to European audiences in her stage
performances. She could write different sentences in
French, German and English at the same time, and

ambidextrously draw landscapes. She was able to write with her mouth as well as both her hands and feet. Using ten pieces of chalk mounted on long pointers attached to each of her fingers she could write ten different figures at the same time. Using a nickname 'The Woman With Ten Brains', she performed for the likes of Woodrow Wilson, Maxim Gorky and Kaiser Wilhelm II.

Arthur Lloyd

Aka 'The Humorous Human Card Index', this early 20th-century entertainer from Massachusetts began his life in the public eye by asking audiences to mention any playing card they wished, whereupon he would produce the said card from his waistcoat. In subsequent years he developed his act to such an extent that he was able to produce on demand such items as insurance policies, war bonds, pawn tickets, alimony waivers, bus transfers, Irish Sweepstake tickets, admission cards to The White House, ringside tickets to boxing matches and even licences to sell opium. Lloyd's clothing was estimated to weigh anything between 45 and 110 pounds. His pockets not only had subdivisions but also subdivisions of subdivisions. He also had a phenomenal memory as he carried up to 15,000 items on his person and was able to summon up any one of them without seeming to search for it.

Seamus Burke

Performance artist who set himself up as the antithesis
to the famous escapologist Harry Houdini. Describing
himself as an 'enterologist', in Manchester in 1935 he
entered a trunk which had previously been locked, tied
with rope and sealed with wax. He went on to appear
inside a sealed tissue bag that was handed to him after
he had been bound mummy-like from head to toe with
more than a hundred feet of stout rope. Claiming to
achieve such stunts by dint of psychic powers, he also
claimed that one night when he took up a pencil it
moved of its own accord across the page in front of
him, drawing strange pictures of birds' faces and
insects' eyes. The next morning when he woke up he
found over 50 such paranormal drawings in front of
him. Such was his fame, he performed in front of the
likes of Hitler, Gandhi, King George and General
Montgomery, and even received an apostolic
benediction from The Pope.

Harry Kahne

Early 20th-century 'mental marvel' who was able to
write five different words simultaneously with pieces
of chalk held in each hand, each foot and also his
mouth. Sometimes he performed this unique task
suspended upside down over blackboards. He could
also compose magic squares at will, add up to five 12
digit numbers in his mind and read newspapers
upside down. He performed to huge audiences in the
States before his death in 1955. He was once asked

what was the population of Manchester and he responded immediately, '735,551', which was the exact answer.

Jose Luis Astoreka

Won a competition for cracking walnuts in his anus in the Basque village of Kortezubi in Spain in 1990. His tally was 30 walnuts in 57 seconds. His brother came second with a similar score in 80 seconds.

TRANSVESTITES

Elagabalus

Roman emperor who, like Nero, enjoyed dressing up as a woman, putting rouge on his face and necklaces on his tunic. He sometimes wore a hairnet as well, and painted his eyes with alkanet. He considered castrating himself, and pleaded with physicians to turn him into a woman. When they resisted, he settled for circumcision as a consolation.

Lord Cornbury

Eighteenth-century governor-general who was both Queen Anne's cousin and her representative in America. It was a role he took literally, dressing up as her for certain functions, and wearing a hoop dress and head-dress for good measure. He was recalled to England in 1708 and immediately arrested: not for transvestism but for a failure to pay his debts. A profligate spender, he was also tight-fisted, and so mean to his wife that she was forced to steal. Despite all this, in 1711 he was made a member of Her Majesty's Privy Council.

Miranda Stuart (1795-1865)

This plucky lady was determined to enter medicine at a time when women weren't allowed to be doctors. When she was 15 she dressed up as a man, calling herself James Barry, and trained to be a doctor. She later joined the British Army and served all over the world. She had a thriving medical career, rising eventually to the position of Inspector General of Hospitals. She campaigned tirelessly for an improvement in the administration and hygiene levels in hospitals, even having the gall to criticise Florence Nightingale on these two counts. It was only after her death that her true identity was discovered, Britain's first female MD had even given birth to a child at one point of her life, without any of her colleagues knowing.

Mary Walker (1832-1919)

Female physicians were thin on the ground in the U.S. in the 19th century, but Walker showed how good they could be at the battle of Gettysberg during the Civil War where she saved the lives of hundreds of Union soldiers and was grudgingly admired by those of a chauvinist persuasion. A suffragette to her fingertips, she dressed in frock coats and trousers like a man and protested passionately against such female attire as corsets and the hoop skirt, which she felt better befitted French prostitutes and were also incitements to sexual attacks. She then launched a campaign against dresses with tight waistlines, which, she believed, damaged the ovaries and fallopian tubes and caused barrenness in women. She was also opposed to nicotine and whenever she passed somebody smoking on the street she knocked the cigarette out of their mouth with her umbrella.

J. Edgar Hoover (1895-1972)

The U.S. president was both a transvestite and a homosexual. Acquaintance Susan Rosensteil says she once saw him dressed up in a fluffy black dress with flounces, lace stockings, high heels, make-up, a curly wig and false eyelashes. Later in the evening she said he read the Bible to two boys who 'worked on him' with rubber gloves. Another night he was spotted in a red dress with a black feather boa round his neck. He had a 40-year relationship with FBI colleague Clyde Tolson but to detract attention from his homosexual nature he launched a vicious campaign against gays. He was also virulent in his tirades against pornography, branding anyone who read *Playboy* as a 'moral degenerate' but he himself loved to watch pornographic films in the aptly-named Blue Room in the FBI offices.

Ernest Hemingway (1899-1961)

An unwitting transvestite, Hemingway was dressed as a little girl for the first three years of his life because his mother had wanted a sister for her first child Marcelline. Many have speculated that his subsequent macho posturing came about as an over-reaction to this. He strenuously objected to photographs from this time being published and threatened his mother that he would withdraw his financial help if she ever released them.

Ed Wood (1924-78)

Wood wrote over 70 pornographic novels but is primarily remembered today for his truly awful movies, such as *Plan 9 from Outer Space*, which have attained a cult following among lovers of camp trash. When he was young he was dressed as a girl by his mother. In time he went on to quite like the idea – which posed certain problems when he was serving with the Marine Corps in the Pacific during the Second World War. He wore female attire under his military garb, and actually managed to win many awards for his bravery in combat. It was just as well he was never wounded, he told a friend afterwards, as it would have been rather difficult trying to explain his bra and pink panties to the army doctor.

VANITY

Pauline Bonaparte (1780-1825)

Napoleon's sister used to bathe daily in five gallons of milk. She was said to be so vain she died with a mirror in her hand.

Elizabeth I of Austria (1837-98)

This excessively vain Austrian Empress could have been accused of spending more time beautifying herself than ruling. She spent a few hours a day having her hair brushed and flew into a tantrum if even one strand fell on the floor during the process. Her hairdressers were forbidden to wear rings on their fingers for fear these would catch in her glorious mane. Neither were they allowed to have long nails. After the brushing was finished the process of shampooing began. The shampoo comprised a mixture of 20 bottles of French brandy and the yolks of a dozen eggs.

So conscious was Elizabeth of her appearance that whenever she was going hunting she had her personal tailor sew the skirt of her riding habit to her bodice to enable her to show off her hourglass figure to its best effect.

Bela Lugosi (1882-1956)

In one of his films where Lugosi was playing a mute, he cried out to the director on the set, 'I am a star! Give me more lines to speak!'

Mae West (1892-1980)

Had it written into her contract that nobody but herself would wear white on the sets of her movies. A true prima donna, she hated acting with her co-stars and preferred to shoot scenes on her own and have them do the reaction shots after she had left the studio.

When she was doing the play *Diamond Lil* in London, she made all the other actresses darken their teeth so hers would look brighter by comparison.

Truman Capote (1924-84)

Liked a profile of himself that *Interview* magazine did so much he ended up buying 500 copies of the magazine and wallpapering his apartment with them.

Joan Collins (1933-)

The actress used to balance matchsticks on her eyelids to make them longer.

VIOLENCE

Elagabalus

The ruthless Roman emperor who ruled from AD 218 to AD 222 used to exert his power over his guests by serving them food made of glass, marble or ivory and compelling them to somehow digest it. He also served spiders and lion's dung, and gave poisonous snakes to his courtiers as gifts. On one occasion he showered his guests with rose petals, using so many of them that some of the guests actually suffocated. When he attended other people's functions he often travelled in a wheelbarrow pulled by naked women.

Don Carlos

This 16th-century Spanish prince, son of Philip II, ordered a cobbler to make a pair of shoes for him that had room for a small pistol he wished to put inside them. His father, however, told the cobbler to disregard this instruction. When Don Carlos saw the finished product was too tight to fit the pistols he made the cobbler cut them up into small pieces and then eat them. His ire was provoked in even more dramatic fashion the day some water spilled down on his head from a balcony he was passing and he ordered the execution of the offenders.

Rev. Sydney Smith (1771-1845)

When lecturing in Edinburgh, Smith had a habit of waking any students who nodded off by firing a revolver.

Jack Mytton (1796-1834)

The 19th-century MP fought hounds by behaving like a dog himself, biting them on the nose and elsewhere.

George Sand (1804-76)

During her affair with Franz Liszt she challenged another of his mistresses to a duel to win him from her unequivocally. The weapons she chose were unique: fingernails.

Jean Mallant

Volatile Frenchman who was having a game of billiards one day in 1834 with his friend Marcel Lenfant when a row broke out between them. It became so heated they decided to settle their differences by means of a duel. They then decided they couldn't wait till dawn so chose to throw billiard balls at one another instead. Jean won first throw and hit Marcel between the eyes with a fatal blow.

Caroline Newton

This New York lady bit off the end of the nose of her friend Thomas Saverland in 1837 when he stole a kiss from her. He took her to court but she was acquitted on the grounds that he had provoked her to such an action.

Spike Milligan (1918-)

Once stabbed Peter Sellers with a potato knife in order to be admitted to a psychiatric hospital.

Mayo Methot

Fiery first wife of Humphrey Bogart who threw whiskey bottles at Bogie frequently when he wasn't measuring up to scratch. She fired a gun at him during one altercation, and set the house on fire following another one. Methot hit the headlines when she stabbed him in the back with a kitchen knife. She also slashed her wrists once when suffering from depression, but she didn't die. Booze killed her eventually.

Elvis Presley (1935-77)

Elvis's mind was out to lunch for the last few years of his life, largely due to his addiction to prescription drugs, which meant that most of the time he was like a volcano waiting to erupt. He fired guns willy-nilly at chairs and ceilings, sometimes even holding them to the heads of his bodyguards. He owned a veritable arsenal of them, including 32 handguns, a submachine gun, Thompson rifles and even an assassin's rifle with telescopic sights. He had an obsession with the fact that somebody was going to kill him and sometimes wore a little derringer in his boots when on stage. The bodyguards had orders to kill anyone who took a shot at him as he didn't want anybody going about the place bragging about the fact that they had just killed Elvis Presley.

Ozzy Osbourne (1948-)

This outrageous heavy-metaller describes Black Sabbath as 'first a rock'n'roll band that meddled with drugs and later a drug band that meddled with rock'n'roll.'

One night when he was polluted with drink and drugs he said to his wife, 'Sharon, we've decided you have to die' and then tried to strangle her. He did time in prison for the attack but she didn't press charges, accepting his story that he had no recollection whatsoever of the incident and was virtually out of his mind when he attacked her.

Osbourne brought a dove into a record company executive's office once in an attempt to convince him he had softened, but when he grew unnerved by the tense atmosphere he bit its head off. As a result of this incident, dead animals were pelted at him on stage in subsequent concerts. Once a bat was flung at him. Imagining it to be a rubber toy, he bit into it. It was only afterwards he realised it was a real one and that he would have to have anti-tetanus shots.

Valerie Solanas

Founder-member of SCUM, the Society For Cutting Up Men. Instead of that, she 'merely' shot Andy Warhol in 1968, claiming he was a worthless individual who stole her ideas. He survived the bullet and she was given three years for assault, but over the next ten years she was in and out of psychiatric hospitals for various reasons, the chief of these being a habit of writing threatening letters to people close to Warhol. She even rang Andy himself not long after the shooting to say she would shoot him again if he didn't do various things for her. She wanted him to make her a star by organising a slot on the Johnny Carson show for her, and to give her $25,000 for stealing her ideas. She also wanted the SCUM manifesto published in the *Daily News*. Andy refused all these requests and stepped up his security arrangements in the light of the phone call. Some of his friends said he was never the same man afterwards, that he was always looking over his shoulder for her.

Sandra Kaushas

Stabbed her husband Edward five times in Pennsylvania in 1985 because he refused to get her a pizza during a Miami-New England football game. He offered to get her chicken at half-time but this was unsatisfactory.

WEIRD SCIENCE

Aristotle (384-322BC)

For his entire life held fast to the belief that men had more teeth than women and refused to accept the fact that both sexes have the same amount. Aristotle believed the sole purpose of the brain was to cool the blood rather than think. He also believed that certain living creatures could come to life spontaneously, like maggots from decaying meat or insects from mud.

Claudius Ptolemy

Greek astronomer from the second century BC who not only believed that the earth was the centre of the universe but also that Ireland was the fourth largest island in the world.

Desiderius Erasmus (1469-1536)

Dutch philosopher who believed that catching syphilis was a sign of sophistication and claimed that any man who failed to contract it was *ignobilis et rusticans*, i.e. a base oaf because he was incapable of attracting a woman. Erasmus himself 'nobly' died of the condition.

James Burnett (1714-99)

Eighteenth-century linguist and natural historian from
Scotland who believed that babies were born with
tails, claiming the tailbone resulted from our simian
ancestry. Asked why such tails were never seen in
maternity wards, he said that vigilant midwives
snipped them off when nobody was looking.

William Buckland (1784-1856)

First professor of Geology at Oxford and a fanatical
naturalist, Buckland was also somewhat quirky. To
prove the efficacy of bird droppings as fertiliser he
once used great quantities of it to write the word
'guano' (Spanish for bird droppings) on the lawn of
his Oxford college. His thesis was proved when later
in the summer the word stood out in a lusher green
colour than the grass around it.

Frank Buckland (1826-80)

The naturalist (William's son) believed that inanimate
things had feelings. If a lamp didn't light properly he
insisted it was because it was feeling sulky and he
once kicked his travelling case, accusing it of
laziness.

Archbishop Richard Whateley (1782-1863)

This Protestant archbishop of Dublin fervently believed you could judge a person's character by the shape of their head. If you put a handful of peas on somebody's head, he claimed, and most of them stayed there, it signified that the person wasn't to be trusted.

Robert Baden-Powell (1857-1941)

British general and founder of the Boy Scouts and, with his wife, the Girl Guide movement, Baden-Powell believed he could analyse people's characters by the way they walked. He claimed 50 per cent of women were adventurous with one leg but hesitant with the other, which indicated instability of temperament. He was also convinced that people who walked with their toes turned out were liars.

Bart Hughes

This Dutch mystic claimed in 1962 that having a hole drilled through one's cranium enabled one to reach a higher state of consciousness. Four years later he came to the U.K. hoping to test his theory but was extradited.

Wilbur Glenn Voliva (1870-1942)

This fundamentalist minister believed that the earth

was flat, blithely disregarding any scientific evidence
that suggested otherwise. He agreed that it was circular,
but denied it was spherical. He likened it to a pancake,
with the North Pole at its centre and its outer
circumference a wall of ice which some people
mistook for the South Pole. This wall, he argued,
prevented all the oceans from spilling over and
plunging sailors off the face of the earth and into hell.

Wilbur also regarded it as nonsensical to suggest
that the sun was 93 million miles away. His own
figure was 3000 miles. God made it to light the earth,
he reasoned, and therefore it would be silly to put it so
far away. 'What would you think of a man who built
a house in Zion,' he asked, 'and put the lamp to light
it in Kenosha, Wisconsin?'

Every year Wilbur took an ad in Chicago and
Milwaukee newspapers challenging anybody to
refute his theories – or, as he saw them, facts – and
nobody took him up on the offer. He had less luck
predicting the end of the world, which he variously
speculated would occur in 1923, 1927, 1930 and
1935.

Michael Jackson (1958-)

The pop star was rumoured to have hired a team of
Nobel Prize-winning scientists to develop a potion
that would make him invisible so that he could avoid
the attentions of the press.

WILLS

Ludovico Cortusio

This 15th-century Paduan lawyer threatened to disinherit anyone who wept at his funeral.

Jonathan Swift (1667-1745)

The Irish writer left money in his will for a Dublin mental asylum. If he'd had enough, he joked, he would have commissioned the building of one to cover the whole of Ireland.

Earl of Chesterfield

London aristocrat who died in 1773, leaving some rather unusual stipulations in his will. So averse was he to racing that he prohibited his godson heir from being involved in it in any manner whatsoever, not only the gambling side but even owning a horse or spending a night at Newmarket, 'that infamous seminary of iniquity'. A codicil to the will – a breach of which would have resulted in Chesterfield's heir forfeiting his entire inheritance – also prohibited him from visiting Italy, a country the doughty earl described as 'the foul sink of illiberal manners and vices'.

Heinrich Heine (1797-1856)

The writer who once defined marriage as 'the high sea for which no compass has yet been invented' left his entire estate to his wife, whom he despised. There was only one condition: that she marry again. His reasoning? 'So that there will be at least one man who will regret my death'.

Major Peter Labelliere

British eccentric who died in 1800, leaving instructions in his will that he should be buried face downwards because the world was out of joint and he wished to set it right by the back-to-front positioning of his corpse.

Eugene Sue (1804-57)

When his mistress died she willed him her skin, leaving instructions that he bind a book with it. The French novelist obliged.

The Comtesse de Noailles (1824-1908)

Eastbourne lady who denied her daughter the right to benefit from her will unless she wore white clothes in summer, and avoided lace-up shoes altogether.

Leo Tolstoy (1828-1910)

The Russian author was so frustrated by members of his family queuing up to see which of them would inherit the bulk of his vast estate he eventually wrote his will on the stump of a tree to avoid the possibility of somebody looking over his shoulder.

James Allen

A robber who left orders that after he died his autobiography should be bound in his own skin and presented to one of his victims as a sign of his remorse. His wishes were carried out in 1837.

Carlo Gamba (1890-1982)

Italian who left his home town of Verbicaro in 1913 to seek fame and fortune in the U.S. In 1962 he heard that his brother Giuseppe had sold the family home for $1000 without notifying him. By this time he was rich, having worked day and night since his arrival to make his way to the top. When he died he was worth $500,000. Giuseppe rubbed his hands in glee at the news, expecting an enormous inheritance, but Carlo's will read: 'I leave all my money except five dollars to the town of Verbicaro to build a hospital. These five dollars I leave to Giuseppe so that he can buy a drink and remember that he should never have sold the family house without my consent.'

Rudolph Valentino (1895-1926)

The actor only left his wife a dollar in his will. That nominal sum meant she couldn't contest it.

Colonel Charles Nash

This misogynist, who died at the end of the 19th century, bequeathed an annuity of £50 to the bell-ringers of Bath Abbey in England on the condition that they ring the bells with 'doleful accentuation' from 8 am to 8 pm every year on the date of his wedding anniversary, and with a 'merry peal' every year at the same hours on the date of his death – which released him from the harridan he had married.

John Quincey Murray

Californian magnate who died in 1929, leaving $3000 to two of his grand-daughters on the condition that they forsake 'bobbed hair, rouge, powder, jewellery, dances and movies', and that they also wear their dresses suitably long at both ends. He left a further $1000 to his grandson provided he refused ever to grow a moustache.

Daisy Alexander

This third daughter of sewing machine magnate Isaac Singer was worth $15 million when she died in 1939. She had promised much of this to her solicitor Barry Cohen. He could only find a 30 year old will made by her many years before with no mention of him. He launched a desperate search for the 'real' will throughout her London mansion, even using a mine detector to probe both ceilings and walls for possible hidden vaults. The search yielded nothing, but Cohen was undeterred and went on to employ witch doctors, clairvoyants and even a cultist with a pendulum that stopped when it located a missing item. One of Daisy's servants remembered that she had been very close to her pet parakeet in her last years and, considering he was a fluent talker, Cohen sent off a group of his employees to trace the bird through three subsequent owners – only to discover that it was not only dead but stuffed as well. Eighteen years later, however, on a deserted beach in San Francisco, an unemployed restaurant worker named Jack Wurm picked up a bottle washed ashore by the tide and inside it was a scrap of paper signed by Daisy saying 'I leave my entire estate to the lucky person who finds this bottle and to my attorney, Barry Cohen, share and share alike'.

Edwin Orlando Swain

This New York voice culture specialist died penniless in New York in 1965, leaving the following enigmatic will:

1. I direct that all my creditors be paid except my landlord.
2. I give and bequeath to my good friend, Theodore Weber, my best aluminium tin if I die of anything

but indigestion. In that event, I give him a sad farewell.

3. To my old friend Ann Lewis I give and bequeath Purcell's 'Passing By', which I wrongfully carried away last Christmas.

4. I give and bequeath to my dear friend Mr George Hale the satisfaction of being remembered in my will.

5. To my old pal Mary Ledgerwood I give and bequeath the sum of 35 cents. It's not much but it's the beginning of a Scotch fortune.

6. I leave to my lawyer Huber Lewis the task of explaining to my relatives why they didn't get a million dollars apiece.

Edgar Bergen

Hollywood ventriloquist who left his dummy $10,000 in his will via the Actor's fund to ensure it was kept in good repair after his death.

Ernest Digweed

Portsmouth schoolmaster who died in 1976, bequeathing his estate to one Jesus Christ should He return to earth and provide proof of His identity. If He didn't appear by 2056, Digweed specified that his assets be seized by the State.

Index

INDEX

INDEX

INDEX